THE
COMPLETE
GUIDE TO
HOSPITAL
MARKETING

PATRICK T. BUCKLEY, MPA

THE HEALTHCARE
COMPLIANCE
COMPANY

Patrick T. Buckley, MPA, Author
Gienna Shaw, Senior Managing Editor
Michele Wilson, Executive Editor
Matthew Cann, Group Publisher
Laura Godinho, Cover Designer
Mike Mirabello, Senior Graphic Artist
Michael Roberto, Layout Artist

Leah Tracosas, Copyeditor
Liza Banks, Proofreader
Darren Kelly, Books Production Supervisor
Susan Darbyshire, Art Director
Claire Cloutier, Production Manager
Jean St. Pierre, Director of Operations

Advice given is general. Readers should consult professional counsel for specific legal, ethical, or clinical questions. Arrangements can be made for quantity discounts. For more information, contact:

HCPro, Inc.
P.O. Box 1168
Marblehead, MA 01945
Telephone: 800/650-6787 or 781/639-1872
Fax: 781/639-2982
E-mail: *customerservice@hcpro.com*

HCPro is the parent company of HealthLeaders Media

Visit HCPro at its World Wide Web sites:
www.healthleadersmedia.com, www.hcpro.com, and *www.hcmarketplace.com*

Contents

Acknowledgments

Writing for people who are new to healthcare marketing takes a good deal of patience and self-discipline. Patience because there is a tendency to forget that just because I think what I'm writing is fairly basic, there are many for whom it isn't. Self-discipline because, well, there are so many things that can be written on this subject, but, as with most everything in life, there are also time constraints and other practical limitations. Fortunately, I had the help of professional colleagues and friends who kept me from becoming too impatient or from going too far afield from the intent of this book, which is to provide an overview of the fundamentals of healthcare marketing.

Thanks to Ivy Bennett, Sr., vice president with Harris Bank; Tim Baylor, assistant professor of marketing at East Tennessee State University; Mike Gilpin, vice president of marketing with Blessing Health System; Catherine Szenczy, senior vice president and CIO at Medstar Health; Betsy Midthun, director of marketing with Avera Scared Heart Hospital; Brian Maloney, managing partner of Imaginary Landscape; Susan Helm, director of marketing for surgery at Southern Illinois University (SIU) School of Medicine; and Gary Dunnington, MD, chair of the department of surgery at SIU.

Thanks also to Cheryl Stone, president and CEO of Cheryl Stone and Associates, LTD, a treasured colleague and good friend who has partnered with me in a number of projects; Matt Cockrell, Esq., former college classmate and close friend, for his many practical suggestions; and my sister, Frances Thomas, author and poet, for her unflagging support and insight into the world of writing.

And, of course, thanks to Gienna Shaw, my editor at HealthLeaders Media, for her expert editing and advice, and for holding my hand at times when this task looked insurmountable.

Finally, thanks to all of the great clients who shared their marketing adventures with me and with whom I have been privileged to work.

About the author

Patrick T. Buckley, MPA

 **Patrick T. Buckley, MPA,** is president and CEO of PB Healthcare Business Solutions, LLC, a consulting firm that assists healthcare organizations with strategy, marketing, and management. He has worked with a variety of healthcare organizations across the country. Among the clients for whom he has provided strategic consulting are academic medical centers, healthcare integrated delivery systems, community hospitals (including critical access hospitals and rural hospitals), multidisciplinary physician group practices, faculty practice plans, and healthcare associations. He has more than 25 years of experience in strategic planning, brand and corporate communications consulting, marketing, advertising, and strategic business development for the healthcare industry. In addition, Patrick is a recognized authority on service line marketing organization and marketing planning, particularly in the areas of cardiovascular services, neurosciences, oncology, orthopedics, and women's health.

Prior to founding PB Healthcare Business Solutions LLC, Patrick was president and CEO of Rynne Buckley Marketing and Communications, a nationally acclaimed healthcare marketing and communications agency. Prior to that, he served as the chief strategic planning and business development officer for the

---

State University of New York Health Sciences Center in Syracuse, NY, where he directed and implemented brand and business development for the clinical enterprise. He also served as the chief strategic planning and marketing officer for Loyola University Health System, Chicago. At Loyola, he initiated and directed the strategic planning and marketing program for the health system, and was instrumental in the development of the heart transplant program, the first of its kind in Illinois.

A featured speaker at national healthcare events, symposia, conferences and live Webcasts for organizations such as the Society for Health Care Strategy and Market Development and for HealthLeaders Media, Patrick was awarded the former Alliance for Health Care Marketing's highest achievement award in marketing excellence. He has been a featured writer in *Chicago Hospital News, Spectrum*, and other national publications. He serves on the editorial advisory board of *Healthcare Marketing Advisor*, a well-respected national publication on healthcare trends and strategy published by HealthLeaders Media.

A graduate of the University of Notre Dame, Patrick holds a Master's Degree in public administration from the Maxwell Graduate School for Citizenship and Public Affairs at Syracuse University. He currently resides in southeastern Wisconsin.

Introduction

Another book on healthcare marketing?

When I decided to write a book about the fundamentals of hospital-based healthcare marketing, I was conflicted. I wasn't sure that another book on healthcare marketing could say anything new that hadn't already been said a dozen times before. But then I realized that today's healthcare marketers belong to a new generation. They grew up with different life experiences and world perceptions than the generations before them. Hence, this book is about *reinterpreting* healthcare marketing for hospital-based marketers.

Although the fundamentals are still relevant and the classic "Four Ps" of marketing—product, price, place, and promotion—are still pertinent, today's healthcare marketers, unlike the early pathfinders of the profession, are learning to obliterate the word "traditional" from their lexicon. Members of the new healthcare marketing generation are natural multitaskers who can devise strategies to compete in both brick-and-mortar and virtual healthcare settings. Like the generation of healthcare marketers before them, they are blazing new trails in Internet-based marketing, new media, customer relationship marketing, transparent pricing, and quality as a comparative market advantage. They've gone through life with an "aren't there other ways to do this?" attitude. Today's healthcare marketers are challenging the old tried—and tired—techniques, from market surveys, to marketing plans, to health fairs and screenings. Today's healthcare marketers know that the job is more than press releases and print ads in the local newspaper. They know that building a healthcare organization's brand takes a lot more than that.

This book is not so much a guide to marketing hospitals as it is a guide to marketing when a hospital's services are part of the solution. Much of what happens in healthcare occurs outside the hospital. Hospital-based marketers need to think beyond the four walls of their organization. Hospital services are a significant part of healthcare delivery, of course, but they are low on the potential customer's list of concerns. This book will present the essentials of marketing, but it will also challenge the reader to think beyond the dry principles and explore what's going through the mind of a child who is preparing to undergo radiation treatment for leukemia, for example, or to imagine how it feels to be a physician who has referred a patient for cardiovascular surgery and is waiting for information about that patient's condition.

It is very easy to get bogged down with everyday projects and forget the ultimate reason that we all got into this field: to educate our organizations about our customers' healthcare needs and to facilitate our organization's ability to meet those needs in a respectful manner.

Does this sound a little corny? It should. We are in a business of people and fulfillment of hope. We must guard against adoption of practices and technologies that might work in other industries but are not appropriate in healthcare, where the stakes are much higher. After all, in other industries, people don't die if they don't get the right service at the right time in the right way.

What you'll find in this book . . . and what you won't

This book will present practical insight and knowledge designed to help marketers who are new to hospital and health system marketing or who come to the job from other fields. It is not meant to be an academic treatise filled with theories and jargon, but rather a real-world discussion about the practical concerns of hospital-based healthcare marketing.

In my first job as a healthcare marketer, I reported to a CEO who held a weekly meeting of the executive team, at which each member of the team always seemed to have something profound and wise to say. At one meeting, the CEO started by pronouncing his belief that our medical center was the most preferred of all the healthcare providers in our region, bar none. I came to this meeting prepared with the results of a consumer attitudes and perceptions survey that didn't quite agree with the boss's opinion. So when it was my turn to speak, I sagely asked the CEO, "Sir, on whose survey data is that observation based?" The CEO replied with a fixed stare that burned a hole in my coffee cup (there were no lattes at that time): "*My* survey data—are there any that are more important?"

That morning, I learned two valuable lessons about surviving in the executive jungle that have stuck with me to this day. First, never sit at the head of the table right next to the boss. Second, you can't necessarily change attitudes and perceptions with facts and figures.

As marketers, it is our duty to bring the facts and figures to the table, to replace statements about what we think with statements about what our patients think. This may not always be the popular thing to do, but it is what we are paid to do. At the same time, there are many factors that enter into the decision-making process for managers, consumers, and physicians.

It is my hope that in this book you will find some practical nuggets of marketing wisdom that will help you become a more effective marketer in your particular organization and marketplace . . . and keep you at the executive table. Just remember my advice about sitting up front.

NOTE: Words in **bold face** throughout this book are defined in the glossary section at the end of this book.

Chapter 1

Welcome to the mixed-up world of healthcare marketing

This chapter will:

- Explain how marketing hospitals and health systems is different than marketing other products and services

- Explain how the marketing mix works in the hospital environment

- Delineate the skill sets hospital marketers need to be successful

---

Marketing healthcare is different

As a consumer, would you think it a bit strange if you were looking for a new suit at the department store and none of the suits had a price tag on it? It would seem odd if there was a sign posted above the clothing rack that said, "Suits are subject to contractual adjustments—buyers are responsible for the amount not paid for by their clothing maintenance plan," right? Likewise, would you go shopping for a new car without having any idea of what it really cost, or without any way to compare its features to those of other cars with similar capabilities? And as a business owner, would you let people who are not your employees control the quality of your products and have a significant effect on your ability to create a safe, high-quality environment for your customers?

And how *do* you market a business that, if it is doing a good job, should not be getting repeat business from its customers?

Welcome to the mixed-up world of hospital marketing!

All aspects of traditional marketing functions—product, price, place, and promotion—are a challenge for hospital and health system marketers. In healthcare, so many processes depend on so many people performing so many specialized tasks that it is easy to see why hospital and health system marketers often struggle to explain to people outside of the healthcare field exactly what it is that they do. It's not even easy to get people *inside the organization* to understand what marketing is all about.

The hospital marketer must not only keep up with the latest clinical technology, new healthcare legislation, and healthcare finance trends, but also be an astute educator and mentor to his or her colleagues, helping them to understand the role they play in creating trust, confidence, and value in the minds of their customers.

Healthcare is constantly changing

Hospitals and health systems are affected by political upheaval; changes in government regulations; declines in **reimbursement**; the growth of alternative medicine; the rise of consumerism; an increase in competition from physician-owned specialty hospitals, retail clinics, and other business models; and a host of other complications. In this complex landscape, there's just no guarantee that the marketing approaches that worked last year will continue to work—or even be legal—this year.

Hospitals are not top-of-mind

Further complicating matters is that hospital preference is not a top-of-mind issue for most consumers. In some respects, marketing for a hospital is like marketing for a funeral home: Each must be available whenever the customer needs its services. People don't typically spend a lot of time thinking about where they would like to be buried or which funeral home should handle the arrangements should they die tomorrow. Likewise, people don't always think about where they want to go if they have a heart attack or need to have hip replacement surgery. There are plenty of other things to worry about on a daily basis, so it's safe to assume that people's preference in hospitals is not at the top of their list of concerns. However, when a person does have a health-related event that requires treatment, you definitely want your hospital to be at the top of his or her mind— and you want it to stay there.

The fact is, people form opinions about their local hospital based on stories they hear from their neighbors, relatives, and coworkers, or from first-hand experience. Also, going to the hospital is usually an uncommon, singular experience (unless a person is undergoing chemotherapy or having a second child, for example). That makes it difficult for patients to compare the care they receive at your hospital with the care they received at a competitor's hospital. After all, you can't take your herniated disc to two hospitals to see which one does a better job. This is why hospitals must do everything possible to make a patient's first experience a good one.

Hospitals spend a significant amount of money each year promoting their brand to get it to the top of the consumer's list. But all that money is flushed down the drain if the experience doesn't match the hype. That's why marketers must forever be concerned with patient satisfaction. And you don't gauge that by analyzing quarterly reports; you do it through daily and ongoing monitoring of what's happening with your customers when they encounter your services.

Hospital marketing is reliant on operations

Say a patient is about to have surgery, but her surgeon has not come by to check on her before the operation. She asks an OR nurse if she can see the surgeon, but the nurse tells her the surgeon is very busy and that she shouldn't worry. The patient is then wheeled into the surgery suite, and her surgery is successful. Later, however, she remembers that the surgeon never stopped by to check on her. She mentions this to her friends, family, and primary care physician (PCP) during a follow-up visit, but doesn't mention it in her post-hospital stay patient satisfaction questionnaire.

Imagine that down the hall another patient is complaining to his visiting relative that he can't sleep because of the noise outside his room and frequent staff visits during the night. Also, he says, his door is always ajar despite repeated pleas to close it. Light from the hallways shines in and keeps him awake. His relative complains to one of the nurses, but the nurse says the door must be kept open. The patient will get used to the noise, she adds dismissively.

Are these examples of breakdowns in hospital operations? Or are they examples of a marketing failure? The answer is "yes" on both counts. If they aren't addressed by both clinicians and the marketing team, these scenarios, which play out frequently in hospitals all over the United States, can hurt patient satisfaction and clinical outcomes by increasing stress for people who are already in a stressful situation. And yet such situations may be dismissed by caregivers, who know the "annoying" patient will be gone soon enough.

Transitioning to healthcare marketing from another industry

In many industries, the marketing department is king. Products are developed with market research before they are engineered, tested, or sold. Marketing and product development are highly integrated, and the experiences of customer targets are infused in every product-line manager's playbook. But this has not generally been the case in hospitals, where operations is often autonomous of marketing and marketing is seen primarily as a source for advertising, publicity, and other forms of promotion. Since the 1980s, when healthcare marketing began to take root, hospital and health system marketers haven't typically been an integral part of the product development process. They are usually brought in to research a new service or promote an existing service line. But rarely do hospital and health system marketers initiate new clinical programs or process improvements. One reason for this is that few hospital marketers have served in a position in which they were directly responsible for managing the delivery of care services. Most have not worked in situations in which they were face to face with consumers and patients. Thus, service line directors and nurse managers do not see why marketers should focus on product development. Whether hospital marketers should be more involved in product development may be debated, but those who are involved have a much better appreciation for the challenges that providers face than those who aren't.

Learn a new definition of marketing

The classic definition of **marketing** is that it is a process of exchange in which willing customers pay a certain price that they believe represents the value of the product or service from which they are seeking to benefit. Go to any department store, retail outlet, or grocery store and you will find products that are marked with a price. Even with non–hard goods marketing (i.e., services), the price for a haircut or a car wash may vary depending on the features or customization that the customer chooses, but before he or she makes the purchase, he or she knows what it is going to cost.

With few exceptions, however, it is nearly impossible for the consumer to make a price/value judgment when it comes to healthcare services. Unlike when consumers comparison-shop for prices when buying a new car or planning a vacation in Hawaii, patients have had no way to compare the costs of hernia surgery, for example, among healthcare providers. Historically, consumers have had no reason to care about the cost of their healthcare for the following reasons:

- **Third-party insurance coverage masks the real cost of healthcare from consumers.** Every year at tax time, I ask my neighborhood pharmacist for a printout of my pharmaceutical purchases for the previous year. And every time I get the printout, it tells me how much money my drug plan paid on my behalf. If I had to pay the full price of the generic drugs alone, I would probably be eating cereal for dinner. Other than paying for their deductibles and copayments, most insured consumers have no idea of the actual cost of their hospitalization because it is masked by third-party reimbursement. Even when they have to pay a 20% share of a $50,000 surgical operation, consumers still do not choose a hospital based primarily on price (although this may change as more employers, in an effort to cut costs, institute higher deductibles and coinsurance and as health savings accounts become more popular).

- **Consumers use healthcare services infrequently.** Because most people are not admitted to a hospital on a routine basis, it is difficult for consumers to make comparisons about one hospital's capabilities versus another's.

                    The Complete Guide to Hospital Marketing

Ratings companies, such as HealthGrades in Golden, CO, J.D. Power and Associates in Westlake Village, CA, and the federal government's ratings Web site, *www.hospitalcompare.com*, are trying to provide consumers with a standardized means for comparing the results of common treatments. The Centers for Medicare & Medicaid Services (CMS) has promulgated the Hospital Consumer Assessment of Healthcare Providers and Systems (HCAHPS), a standardized patient satisfaction survey designed to give consumers an objective means for making comparisons among hospitals in terms of their quality. However, so long as physicians admit patients to hospitals at which they have privileges, the consumer is still limited in his or her choice as to where to be hospitalized.

By now it should be abundantly clear that hospital marketing is different. So how do you translate what you know about marketing to the world of hospital and healthcare marketing?

As noted earlier, marketing involves an exchange process of some sort. Classic definitions often talk about marketing in terms of the "Four Ps"—product, place, price, and promotion. In 2004, the American Marketing Association adopted the following definition of marketing, according to its Web site:

An organizational function and a set of processes for creating, communicating, and delivering value to customers and for managing customer relationships in ways that benefit the organization and its stakeholders.

That definition is accurate—albeit not exactly easy to explain to someone when they ask what it is that you do for a living. For people who live and breathe this stuff every day and who are adapting marketing principles to an industry that has misunderstood the role of the marketing discipline for years, I would like to offer up the following definition of *healthcare marketing*:

> *Healthcare marketing is educating ourselves as to the wants and needs*
> *of our potential customers, and, based on the knowledge we gain,*
> *educating our customers and offering them valued services that fulfill*
> *their needs when and where they need those services.*

Notice this definition doesn't include the words *exchange, product, pricing, distribution (place),* or *promotion.* And yet the Four Ps are in there. The emphasis is on educating ourselves (through market research), educating our customers (through promotion), and offering services (our products) such that they are valued (the price/value exchange) and fulfilled (that's distribution).

Meet a new kind of customer

So now that we have a working definition of healthcare marketing, let's explore the idiosyncrasies of the marketing mix as it is encountered by the healthcare consumer. But first, let's be clear as to who our customers are. For hospital-based marketers:

> ***Customers*** *are individuals and groups of individuals who utilize our*
> *services, either to enhance delivery of their own services or to satisfy*
> *a healthcare-related need.*

Under this definition, our customers can be both business to business (B2B) and business to consumer (B2C) and can include:

- Physicians on our medical staff (B2B)

- Physicians who refer patients to physicians on our medical staff for diagnosis/treatment (B2B2B)

- Consumers who utilize our services as patients (B2C)

- Managed care plans (B2B)

- Employers (B2B)

Hospitals have numerous other constituencies, such as those affiliated healthcare organizations or hospitals with which they have patient transfer agreements, cancer or heart disease support groups, emergency medical providers, and community organizations that meet at the hospital, for example. In fact, anyone or any group who can benefit from the hospital's services can become a customer. But for the most part, the primary customers with whom you will be dealing are physicians and patients. Examples of the wants and needs of the customers are shown in Figure 1.1.

Figure 1.1 Wants and needs of hospital-based customers

Common healthcare customer groups:	What each group generally wants or needs:
Medical staff	Information on patients who have been admitted to the hospital Information on hospital services Access to medical records Up-to-date technology
Referring physicians	Improved health outcome for patients Timely reports Return of patients to the physician's care Prompt access to consults Involvement in comanaging the follow-up of patients
Consumers	Availability and access Information to make decisions Confidence in diagnosis and treatment
Patients	Quick return to health Continuous communication Confidence in care protocols Convenience in scheduling visits, test, procedures TLC (tender loving care) Involvement of spouse/partner Options, pros and cons
Managed care	Managed utilization of procedures, controlled cost, member satisfaction, outcome measurement

Rethink product organization and delivery

Historically, hospitals were organized around medical-surgical and intensive care, the emergency room, radiology, laboratory, pharmacy, and a series of support services (e.g., laundry and central sterile supply maintenance). Each area operated as a diagnosis, treatment, support, or ancillary service (non–medical-surgical care, such as emergency care). A patient would be admitted to a medical or surgical care wing of the hospital and would experience numerous interventions by hospital staff and physicians from different departments. Nursing staff on various floors of the hospital were responsible for carrying out physicians' orders, while hospital administrators were mostly assigned to provide supervision over clinical, professional, and support services. A patient's hospitalization regimen was determined solely at the discretion of the patient's attending physician. Reports for hospital administration focused on patient days by physical unit. Bills were generated based on the hospital's charges, which varied according to the length of the patient's stay, the type of unit the patient spent time in, specific diagnostic and treatment interventions, and the various drugs administered. Charges were paid in what was called "cost plus reimbursement."

Then, in 1982, Congress passed the Tax Equity and Fiscal Responsibility Act (TEFRA), a major bill affecting Medicare reimbursements. Medicare began to pay hospitals a fixed rate (with adjustments for local area wages) for categories of care. In hospital parlance, these are referred to as **diagnosis-related groups** (DRG). Thus, to maximize their payments from Medicare, it behooved hospitals to keep costs down by shortening lengths of stay where medically appropriate and by performing only those tests and procedures absolutely necessary for diagnosis and treatment. This payment system, with annual adjustments and tweaks, is still the principal basis for the way hospitals organize and deliver their services.

In the mid- to late-1980s, with an eye toward saving costs and building profitable patient volume, hospitals began looking at how other industries developed and delivered their products and services. Hospital-based services began to be organized into what are called **service lines,** a term borrowed from manufacturing industries that promote product lines (see Figure 1.2). Service lines are an attempt to bring the concept of strategic business units into hospital management. In simple terms, the idea behind service line management is to bring all

---

of the production components involved in the delivery of a care process into one management chain of command that is typically led by a service line director. For example, all of the major components involved in the delivery of cancer care are managerially organized within the oncology service line. Because there is natural crossover of disease processes (e.g., brain cancer crosses neurosciences with oncology, pediatric heart surgery crosses pediatrics with cardiovascular surgery), service lines are often marketed through a multidisciplinary approach that requires the service line director to "buy" services from other service lines and from support services.

Figure 1.2   Clinical services are packaged and managed as a strategic business unit

What used to be referred to as simply:	May now be marketed as:	And may involve these specialties:
Cardiovascular patients on a medical-surgical unit	The Heart Care Institute	Cardiology, surgery, pulmonary, imaging, rehabilitation
Minor emergency care	Fast Track/Prompt Care	Internal medicine, family medicine, consulting sub-specialties
Orthopedics	The Bone and Joint Institute	Orthopedics, immunology and rheumatology, physical medicine, physical therapy
Gynecologic care	The Breast Care Center	Medical oncology, surgical oncology, radiotherapy, mammography

The marketing department provides technical assistance to each of the service lines, such as market research, marketing planning, and promotion. But the service line director is responsible for all aspects of the overall service—ensuring that services are what they should be, that customers receive the best possible care, and that the service line is profitable.

Prepare for a new role in pricing

Hospital pricing is undergoing a sea change. As cost accounting systems become more precise, and as the true cost of care is reflected in charges (as opposed to pricing set by cross-subsidization, in which certain services are priced more than they cost because they are reimbursed better than other services), hospital pricing will hopefully become more understandable to consumers.

Historically, hospital marketers have had an almost nonexistent role in setting prices. This task has always been under the purview of the CFO. However, as more and more services are not covered by insurance (which means patients must pay for them out of their own pockets), hospital marketers are increasingly getting involved in pricing issues.

Health plans have attempted to make consumers more accountable for their use of services by making it more costly for them to access physicians outside of a prescribed network. Marketing elective services such as bariatric surgery, LASIK eye surgery, ultra-fast CT scanning, and mammography must be price-sensitive for consumers. The marketing strategy for promoting such services must be highly targeted and take into account that not everyone who can afford them is willing to pay for them out of pocket.

One way marketers can become more involved in pricing is by testing price sensitivity for elective services through focus groups and consumer surveys. Consumers are learning to ask how much a procedure will cost and to postpone procedures or look for alternative approaches to cut down on out-of-pocket expenses. And as physicians become increasingly able to perform ambulatory procedures from their own facilities, offering patients a more convenient and comfortable setting, hospital marketers must monitor consumers' out-of-pocket costs and determine an appropriate differentiating marketing strategy. Will you set your organization apart for its excellent outcomes? Stellar safety? The expertise and experience of its specialists?

One large urban hospital I worked with found through focus groups that consumers in the area felt that if the hospital offered services for free, such as health screenings, that it must have a lot of money, whereas a hospital that charged a reasonable fee was likely to be more caring. The same focus groups also felt that, if making a choice between one hospital charging $125 for a healthy heart exam and another charging $50, they were more likely to pay the higher cost because that hospital was "higher quality." After tinkering with various price levels, the

hospital found that it actually attracted more people by charging more for services than it did with its historic underpricing.

Understand the patient pathway

It is very important for marketers to be aware of the decision-making process that consumers and physicians go through when choosing a hospital. Before a person ever steps into a hospital, he or she makes a number of decisions that eventually lead to a hospitalization. The patient pathway (see Figure 1.3) shows how a person with a heart problem, for example, accesses the hospital from entry (through referral to a cardiologist by his or her PCP or admission directly through the emergency department) through post-hospitalization follow-up.

Figure 1.3   Understanding the patient pathway

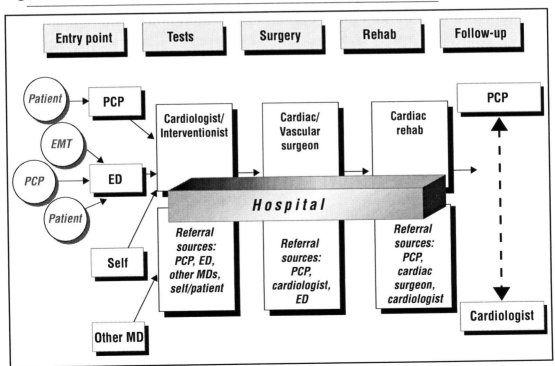

This is where brand advertising can be most effective—building awareness and preference for an organization so that when a patient needs services, the hospital is on his or her short list of preferred providers. Of course, the PCP is still a patient's most important source of hospital information. And sometimes a patient has little choice about which hospital he or she goes to—his or her physician may be affiliated with only one hospital, for example—and health plans also sometimes limit patients' choices.

Once the PCP determines that the patient needs medical care, the patient may receive a referral from the PCP or self-select a cardiologist based on a referral from a friend, family member, coworker, or another source. The patient may also enter the continuum of care through the emergency department. The marketing interaction in this scenario occurs at three key points: between the PCP and the specialist to whom the PCP makes the referral, between the patient and the cardiologist's office, or between the prehospital EMT/paramedic and the hospital emergency department.

The hospital marketer's role in these referral processes is governed by the particulars of the consumer's or provider's situation. For example, it may start with a patient contacting the hospital's call center looking for a referral to a cardiologist, or it may start when marketing arranges for a hospital-sponsored continuing medical education program on cardiovascular advances for primary care physicians. Or it could start via the Web—such as through an online cardiac risk assessment tool on the hospital's Web site. Regardless of the means, however, it is most important that marketing map the process and determine the key points of interaction and what happens at each of those points. By doing this, potential communication mishaps can be avoided and customer expectations can be better met.

Promoting hospital services

Let's be clear about one thing: Accessing the healthcare system is emotionally draining for the patient and for his or her friends and family. Visiting a hospital is never a person's first choice of how to spend his or her time. Patients lose their privacy, entrust their bodies to strangers they may never meet again, and have no guarantee that they will come out of the experience well—or even that they will come out of it alive.

You probably wouldn't want to buy a pizza if it came with a warning label stating, "Eating this pizza could result in death" (even though if you eat enough pizza it probably will). Yet patients who are about to have surgery must sign a consent form that includes a statement about the possibility of death, even if the chance of that happening is remote.

Hospital marketers know that each patient's experience is unique and that advertising must connect emotionally with consumers. Likewise, the stories we tell about patients or physicians must portray the hospital as a place that respects individuals and empathizes with their lack of control over their situation. Yet so much of hospital and health system advertising is focused on showing the newest imaging equipment or life-saving technology. Almost every marketer I work with wants to achieve the "high-touch/high-tech" duality in advertising. Healthcare advertising works, it's true—but if it doesn't make an emotional connection with consumers, it's better to put the money to other uses.

Matrix and consensus management

There is another aspect of healthcare marketing that often takes those new to the field by surprise: the culture of making decisions by committee and of endless committee meetings. Those who come to healthcare marketing from for-profit, especially retail, businesses, are often frustrated by the decision-making processes and the influence of "nonmarketing" people on their work. One of the biggest complaints I hear from marketers who have come from other industries is about the number of stakeholder meetings they must attend and the number of presentations they must make to committees before they can get a go-ahead for a marketing initiative. Marketers from other industries are used to having the autonomy to make decisions without mass consensus. Indeed, in most hospitals and health systems, there are few opportunities for marketers to make unilateral decisions.

The other characteristic of healthcare marketers that's unfamiliar to marketers from other industries is that bringing in business does not earn healthcare marketers the same kind of traction that it does in sales-driven industries. In fact, yet another unique aspect of this industry is that healthcare organizations are often concerned about not being able to handle patient volume as a result of a marketing campaign (a "problem" many businesses would be happy to have).

It's great to be able to tell your organization's leaders that market share of a particular service line increased 2% as a direct result of your marketing initiatives. But your CEO will greet that news by asking what that growth cost in terms of new technology and additional staff, your CFO will want to know about payer mix and contribution margin, the chief medical officer will be concerned about the effect of the new business on quality of care, and the chief nursing officer will ask about the OR's capacity to handle additional volume. Further, it's not unusual for physicians to tell you that they see enough patients every day, thank you, and that they aren't interested in seeing more.

Hospital-based marketers tread a fine line between answering the demand for **return on investment** (ROI) of the money spent on marketing and the political realities of working in an environment in which the product (physician care) and the distribution channels (often physician-directed) are not in their control. To be effective, hospital-based marketers must build in additional time to achieve buy-in for their marketing plans from the rest of the organization, and they must be aware that their ability to achieve results is only as good as the organization's operational performance. Timely scheduling of appointments, quality service, and clinical competence all play a major role in the marketer's ability to achieve sustained business growth.

It's the relationships, stupid!

Healthcare marketing is all about relationships. And relationships take time to cultivate. CEOs will come and go, but the more successful ones realize early on that they must involve physicians in the decision-making process. One CEO I have worked with moved his office next to the medical staff lounge to be more accessible. Rather than abuse the privilege, the medical staff respected his open-door policy and only used it for major concerns. This action was in sharp contrast to the prior CEO's setup—his office was hidden away and the entrance to it blocked by three secretaries.

Likewise, to build those relationships, marketing professionals must also make themselves available. Some of the best intelligence comes not from market share reports but rather from impromptu meetings in the hallway. One effective marketing director I know makes it a daily practice to stop by the hospital switchboard (now referred to as a call center) to let staff members there know what was happening that day and to ask them if there was anything that might make them more effective when answering calls. This recognition of their importance enhanced their productivity and gave the marketing director valuable information regarding the types of calls coming in on a real-time basis. Likewise, if you have greeters in the lobby, or a valet parking service, it will pay dividends to visit these employees and other frontline staff daily.

Focus on simplicity

As healthcare marketing continues to evolve, the danger exists that technology and marketing innovations will obfuscate what is and will always be a personal experience. Contrary to popular belief, automated voicemail at the hospital's call center does not simplify processes like it does when ordering a prescription refill at the pharmacy. People generally don't telephone the call center for routine reasons—they call when they need to contact a doctor, get information about a loved one's condition, or schedule a medical test or procedure. Think about all the times you have called a business and were frustrated because you did not get a human response. Then think how even more frustrating it would be if you were trying to get a hold of your physician while worrying about the pain of a bleeding ulcer.

Nor does overblown advertising play a role in building and sustaining trust, confidence, and dependability. "Wait," you may say. "You can't build trust unless you let people know what it is you do." True, but that's not the point. Consider the pitcher in baseball. You can have a great lineup of hitters, but if your pitching is poor, all the hitting in the world will not win ballgames. Focusing on simplifying the consumer experience and delivering great service will win you more ballgames than making clever television commercials.

        The Complete Guide to Hospital Marketing

Follow the money?

I was having a cup of coffee with a colleague of mine who works as the director of facilities planning at an esteemed academic medical center in the Midwest. Not surprisingly, we got on to the subject of where the future of healthcare delivery was heading. How much heart surgery would eventually become outpatient-based? Would the generally horrible eating habits of baby boomers mean that we should be planning for diabetes hospitals, just as there are heart hospitals today? My friend took a sip of coffee, put down his cup, looked me straight in the eye and said, "Pat, providers will do what they think is going to be reimbursed. Behavior always follows the money."

I was struck by what I thought was a rather crass observation. Wasn't the aim of healthcare to get people well through the most appropriate treatment and protocols? Weren't doctors and hospitals supposed to provide the right care, in the right amount, and with the right equipment, regardless of how such measures were reimbursed? But then I realized that there was truth in what my colleague had said. Healthcare delivery has always been influenced by such factors as whether the patient's insurance plan will cover a particular procedure and reimbursement rates. Although the aim of this book is not to debate the fairness or the inequities of the U.S. healthcare system, it is important for marketers to anticipate the likely action of payers when they are designing marketing strategies and follow the subsequent behavioral trends of providers.

Summary

- Marketing in a hospital environment has unique challenges that are not found in most other organizations. The product is variable, the customer is not usually a willing buyer, and there is not a true price value exchange.

- The skills that are critical for the marketing professional are both quantitative and qualitative. A critical skill is the ability to achieve consensus among the players involved in the delivery of a clinical service or customer interaction. Marketers must display skills in market research, and team play is very important.

- Marketers must integrate themselves into the hospital's operations to truly understand the interaction between producers and consumers.

You be the marketer

You have just accepted a position as the chief marketing officer at Sunnyside Memorial Hospital. You've met with the CEO, the COO, the CFO, the chief medical officer (CMO), and the chief nursing officer (now commonly called the senior vice president of clinical services). Each has told you what he or she thinks are the priorities for the year, but from your interviews you discern that there is no coherent approach to program development. The CFO feels that there is a need for marketing to increase profits, while the CMO thinks marketing is superficial largely because the former marketing director focused on "we're a top 100 hospital" advertising. From your early assessment of the service lines, you feel that there are operational issues that need to be addressed before market share can be increased. The COO has stated her belief that marketing has no role in program development or operational improvement. How will you manage the diverse

You be the marketer (cont.)

expectations of your fellow C-suite officers? How will you integrate marketing with operations?

Assess your relationship with the service line management structure in your organization. Determine how you can enhance your effectiveness with each of the directors.

Pick one major service line and audit the patient pathway.

Get out of your office! Walk through the main entrance of your hospital as if you were looking through the eyes of someone who has never been to your hospital before. What do you see? Is there a friendly face to greet you? Talk to frontline staffers—valet parkers, volunteer greeters, people behind the information desk. Ask them about the patient (and visitor) experience. If they were in charge, what would they do differently?

Chapter 2

Healthcare marketing information and market planning

This chapter will:

- Help the marketer better understand how and when to use internal and external market information

- Explain the importance of proactively designing a marketing information system that is managerially meaningful

- Discuss the challenges inherent in tracking return on investment of marketing dollars

- Provide the marketer with a framework for assisting service line directors with market planning

The evolving state of healthcare information management

If you are new to healthcare marketing, you will soon learn that the information you need to draw a composite picture of your service area is much harder to come by than it is in other businesses. Even though healthcare is a multibillion-dollar industry, historically, hospitals have operated as a cottage industry. Marketers in industries other than healthcare are used to sharing a significant

---

amount of competitive intelligence, something that is still emerging in healthcare marketing. In the auto industry, for example, the major manufacturers have shared data for decades, resulting in uniformity of suppliers' specifications and enhancement of consumers' ability to compare prices, performance, quality, and safety. It is likely that a consumer will ask more questions about performance and safety when looking to buy a car than when he or she is about to have his or her chest cracked open for quadruple bypass surgery.

The toy industry, like the healthcare industry, is subject to numerous federal regulations. In response, it has developed voluntary safety standards that make it almost impossible for a toy to be marketed without its having first passed stringent safety tests and requirements. In healthcare, on the other hand, best practices are only just beginning to be shared industrywide. As a group, hospital marketers need to get past the fear of sharing competitive intelligence and push their organizations to support data sharing to make it possible for consumers to compare hospitals on a level playing field.

With all the focus today on Internet-enabled technologies, electronic medical records, and quality and safety improvements, healthcare is a burgeoning IT playground. And yet it can still be a struggle to get such basic information as the number of procedures performed by a particular physician and the outcomes of his patients.

Given that the majority of physicians are office-based and there is no universal database for office-based procedures, one can only go by word-of-mouth or reputation when judging a physician's quality performance. Until healthcare information reporting crosses the full continuum of subacute, acute, chronic care, alternative medicine, and office-based procedures and services, marketers will have an incomplete picture of their constituents' healthcare needs and will continue to rely on imperfect sources of information to make business decisions.

Enter the healthcare marketing information system. Healthcare information businesses have mined years of health insurance claims data, Medicare claims, and cost reports and have married this information with demographic modeling software that enables marketers to project the potential number of hospitalizations and outpatient visits in a geographic area by gender and age group. These information companies purchase state and Medicare data to help their clients research their markets. The data are populated by the **diagnosis-related group** (DRG) utilization reports submitted by all hospitals to their state healthcare departments.

By rolling up the data by **service line** (which is defined by a grouping of related DRGs), modeling software makes it possible to estimate what a hospital's market share for a particular disease or procedure might be.

The challenge for the healthcare marketer is to know what information is meaningful and what isn't. Information is meaningful if it fosters strategic decision-making; otherwise, it is just data (and not information). Many hospital marketing departments do not proactively design marketing information systems. Instead, they depend on a number of sources to get their information and then cobble together reports that contribute marginally to new program development. A chief weakness of hospital marketing information systems is that market share measurement often lags by a year or more, and the biannual consumer preference survey does not match current market behavior.

It is important that a marketing information system is designed to be more than a tool to measure market share trends and track patient volume trends. The marketing department should take the lead in working with operations and IT to build a marketing information system that produces the type of reports that service line leaders require to deliver needed and profitable services now. Figure 2.1 shows the type of information that the marketer should be working with for oncology service line planning: the specific questions for which information is needed, the sources of information, and the reports that should be generated.

Figure 2.1 Basic elements of marketing information system

Key questions	External data/sources	Internal data/sources
How do our clinical offerings compare with our competitors?	**Primary data:** Consumer household survey research	Finance/business office
		IT/medical records
Where are we gaining/losing market share?	Focus group research	Medical staff office
What is the potential for cancer utilization in our service area?	**Secondary data:** Market share reports	ER
		Patient admitting call center
	State hospital association databases	DRG case mix
What is the profile of the cancer service line with respect to:	American Cancer Society and state cancer society use rates by body organ	Physician productivity reports
		Financial analysis
- Referral sources	U.S. Census	Referral sources
- Profitability	State department of public health statistics	Cancer registry
- Program offerings		
- Technology	Outpatient claims data	
- Provider capabilities		

                                        The Complete Guide to Hospital Marketing

Market research and analysis

Market research and analysis includes **primary** and **secondary market research**.

Primary market research involves seeking information generated from sources other than the hospital's internal reporting systems and from externally generated reports. It includes quantitative (research data that are projectable) and qualitative (research data that are not projectable) methodologies, and information can be gathered through a number of vehicles, such as consumer household surveys, physician surveys, mall intercepts, focus groups, personal interviews, and Internet-based surveys.

Conversely, **secondary market research** refers to already existing information obtained from the hospital's internal departments or from organizations that have compiled and processed data for a particular purpose. This type of research is often utilized to develop management reports on productivity; volume, population, and financial trends; market position; and physician productivity. Examples include market share reports and incidence and prevalence rates compiled by local, state, federal, and private healthcare agencies and associations.

When to use qualitative and quantitative research

Qualitative research is most beneficial for testing concepts, products, and ideas with consumers through focus groups. Quantitative research is used when it is more important to track changes in consumer attitudes or behavior over time. Quantitative surveys provide a measurement baseline and make it possible to project results, whereas qualitative research is not projectable but has the advantage of eliciting ideas and attitudes that are not attainable through quantitative research.

Measuring marketing-driven ROI

One area of marketing measurement that has become a huge focal point is analysis of **return on investment** (ROI). You can't be in the hospital marketing business long before you hear the question that provokes terror in the hearts of those who can't answer it: *"How will this marketing project contribute the bottom line?"* Much has been written and spoken about this subject, yet although there are increasingly better ways of measuring ROI in healthcare marketing, it is still a fairly elusive goal.

Many organizations require marketers to demonstrate ROI to justify their staffing levels, overhead, and annual budget. Some organizations expect marketing to deliver a 200% return, others 10%, while still others have not set a specific target number. But there's a danger in basing the annual marketing budget on an artificial ROI target because there are several barriers to measuring ROI that are unique to the healthcare industry and many variables that affect healthcare marketing ROI.

Tracking results

Perhaps the most common question about measuring ROI often comes after a campaign has been "out there" for some time and it becomes increasingly difficult to track whether the campaign still brings in patients. Management will often ask whether the people who use the hospital's services wouldn't have come to the hospital regardless of whether they saw the campaign. Further, do you consider patients to be new business if they come to your organization for a new service, even though they have been patients of the hospital for some other need for one or more years prior?

    The Complete Guide to Hospital Marketing

One solution to this problem is to define a "new" patient as one who has not had any medical record activity for the most recent two or three years. Still, counting these people as new patients could be misleading because they may be coming to your hospital for a service that isn't offered at competing healthcare organizations. If their physician isn't affiliated with any other hospital but yours, a referral from that physician that results in a hospital inpatient admission probably can't be attributed to a marketing campaign, either. In both cases, these patients would have come to your hospital regardless of marketing. If you want to measure the ROI of a campaign, it's a good idea to get buy-in about whom to consider a new patient and how to account for patients who would have come to the organization anyway.

Assigning costs

Another hurdle faced by many marketers trying to measure ROI for their efforts is when the organization's indirect costs are assigned to the marketing department in addition to its direct overhead costs. Many a campaign appears to be profitable until those deadly indirect costs are assigned. If it is fair to assign a certain percentage of indirect costs to marketing efforts, then shouldn't it also be fair that marketing be credited for a percentage of each revenue center's income, either as a result of marketing's direct support or as a result of overall advertising? Again, make sure you define exactly what expenses and what earnings will be considered in the ROI calculation *before* the marketing campaign begins.

Getting the complete picture

A number of consulting firms have developed methodologies to approximate marketing ROI—for example, using call center statistics. These approaches are good for tracking activity that results from a specific event or promotional campaign (e.g., the number of calls to the physician referral line after a health fair

---

exhibit), but because they only focus on promotion and response, they do not create a complete picture of marketing value. In particular, such efforts tend to lack a true picture of the real financial impact of the marketing department. And they also fail to account for omissive marketing—the potential losses in sales that could result from not actively promoting a program, event, or service.

Many hospitals track ROI based on response to an advertising "call to action" or attendance at a special event or health screening. Some call centers have software capabilities or outsource to companies that can track real downstream patient activity and associated net revenue (charges minus contractual adjustments minus direct and indirect costs). In other situations, estimates based on national experience are used to determine the potential net revenue that results from a marketing activity, again applying factors for fixed and variable costs.

All in all, the state of the art of measuring ROI may not be perfect, but ROI measurement is essential if marketers are to justify their expenditures. The more precise and positive the tracking is, the better the chances are for increasing your budget and earning your department the respect it deserves.

The service line marketing plan versus the business plan

The director of cardiovascular services calls. Your conversation with him might go something like this:

Cardio director (CD): "I need a marketing plan for the coming year. How do I go about putting one together?"

You: "Are you looking for a marketing plan, or a business plan?

CD: "What's the difference?"

You: "Well, a marketing plan is focused on achieving specific goals having to do with market share, volume growth, new services development, referral relationships, and customer satisfaction, whereas a business plan is more than that. The business plan includes operational, financial, and staffing considerations, in addition to marketing strategies."

CD: "Well, whatever it is, I need it pretty quick!"

You: "Okay, why don't we plan a meeting of the service line team and start with a market assessment?"

CD: "Sounds good to me."

Confusion often exists over what exactly "marketing" means. As marketers, we must be cognizant of all of the components that go into making a clinical offering successful. We are in the business of creating successful organizations, not successful marketing plans. However, the marketing plan moves us in the right direction. So even though marketing planning is both essential and vital to devising strategies and committing resources, the service line director has responsibility and accountability for ensuring that all the elements that build a business are in place to achieve targeted volumes, profit, and market growth goals.

Key questions a service line marketing plan should answer

The marketing plan should answer the following questions:

- What are the most effective means for building awareness and, ultimately, preference for the selected service line?

- What are the primary channels (e.g., business to business, business to consumer, other) through which customer volume will be generated, and for what percentage of business will each account?

- How do we best target these specific referral channels?

- What are the most effective marketing strategies for delivering the selected clinical services, in whatever venue they are offered?

- How will we measure the effectiveness of our marketing strategies after they are executed?

Marketing teams

Service line marketing teams develop marketing strategies for their respective service lines. Typically, in addition to marketing staff members, the teams include administrative and clinical members, including the service line manager, medical staff representatives, nursing representatives, and other individuals who are directly involved with the delivery of care. It should take two to three meetings for each service line marketing team to develop their specific goals and strategies.

What should the marketing plan include?

The information gained from service line team meetings is distilled and merged into one comprehensive strategic marketing plan. To ensure that everyone is working from the same playbook, each service line should utilize a template provided by the marketing department. The template will likely include the following information:

- **Market profile.** The market profile describes the marketplace dynamics with respect to the service line's market position, its strengths, competitive challenges, and growth opportunities.

- **Clinical program profile.** In the clinical program profile, the capabilities of the provider panel for each service line are fully assessed, along with the delivery of services, including prevention and treatment, care coordination, customer service issues, clinical service interdependencies, referral flow, technology, and any existing or potential affiliations with other healthcare providers.

- **Target market groups.** The appropriate internal and external audiences will be identified and profiled. Internal audiences include staff members and employees, whereas external audiences include area physicians, consumers, patients (current and former), employers and business associations, and payers.

- **Goals and objectives.** Specific goals relating to key result areas (e.g., consumer awareness and preference, volume and market share, quality, and profitability, if available) will be set for each of the priority service lines. Objectives (i.e., success measures) will also be set to measure attainment of the goals. Typically, determining whether objectives have been met involves comparing post-research preference and attitudes to pre-plan implementation baselines, as well as comparing volume numbers and other quantitative measures (e.g., patient and referring physician satisfaction) to the baselines.

- **Strategic initiatives.** Strategies for furthering program development and building referrals by target market group will be formulated. Promotional strategies may include public relations and publicity, special events, community outreach, advertising, direct mail, Web site advertising, and personal selling.

- **Implementation.** Who does what, when, with what resources, and who is accountable for achieving goals?

Summary

- Marketing information systems must be responsive to the needs of service line leadership. Information must be timely, accurate, and relevant to accomplishment of strategic imperatives and/or operational improvements.

- Market planning incorporates primary and secondary market research. Primary research can be both quantitative and qualitative and is derived from original sources; secondary research may be quantitative and qualitative and uses already existing information that was compiled for a particular purpose.

- Market planning is a team activity. Utilizing a team will inculcate ownership and produce better results in the long-term.

You be the marketer

Your CEO wants to know if creating a program for bariatric surgery would be a good investment. She asks you for a marketing plan. You've completed the initial market analysis and demonstrated that, with investment in the required resources, the bariatric surgery program is feasible and can be successful within three years. Now you need a service line business plan—one that includes a well-thought-out marketing plan and addresses these questions:

1. **A need/demand assessment**

   - What are the target demographics?

   - What is the prevalence of candidates for this type of surgery?

   - Who else performs this surgery, where, and what are their numbers and outcomes?

   - What are the key success factors?

2. **An assessment of the financial feasibility**

   - What are the primary cost elements in developing a successful program?

   - What should be the ROI?

You be the marketer (cont.)

- What is breakeven?

- What do the three-year pro forma financial statements indicate?

3. An assessment of operational needs

- How many staff members do we need to manage and support this program?

- Who should be involved?

4. An assessment of regulatory concerns

- Is a "certificate of need" permit required?

- Do we need approval from the state department of health?

5. An analysis of the market.

- How many competitors are there, and what are their strengths and vulnerabilities?

- Are there underserved populations?

Chapter 3

Marketing management

This chapter will:

- Help marketers to optimize the resources they have in order to achieve marketing goals and objectives

- Describe best practices that marketers can adopt

- Explain how to conduct a marketing audit to identify areas that need strengthening

- Give marketers practical tips on project and client management

Healthcare marketing management comes of age in hospitals

For decades, hospitals functioned without formal marketing departments. They focused on what was considered "soft" selling: building good will through the auxiliary league, running feel-good stories in the hospital's community newsletter, and keeping the business side of hospital operations, for the most part, invisible to the public. Fifteen years ago, you didn't use the word "customer" to describe users of hospital services—that was considered the parlance of for-profit, capitalistic enterprises, and not nonprofit providers of healthcare services.

The emergence of the business side of marketing for hospitals was inevitable: Any time you have perfect competition (in economic terms, when no one has a monopoly and can therefore control the price of goods), there will be a need to differentiate yourself from others who offer the same goods and services that you offer. When the federal government flexed its purchasing muscle and did away with cost-plus reimbursement, the age of hospital marketing finally arrived. However, when insurance companies began to see ways to make money by developing products that turned physicians and hospitals into widgets, hospitals seriously began to differentiate themselves through branding, service lines, and centers of excellence.

The hospital marketing structure

Every marketing organization is unique. There is no one model that works for all hospitals. Having consulted with leading healthcare systems across the country, I have observed multimillion-dollar health systems that over-fund and over-staff marketing; yet they do not achieve the level of market share they deserve for those efforts. Conversely, I have worked with small community hospitals with extremely limited marketing dollars that are marketing overachievers, making the most of the finite resources they have at their disposal.

All marketing directors are searching for norms—how large their staff should be, how much they should spend on different types of advertising, what the best marketing organizational structure looks like, and so on. Frankly, I cringe whenever I see marketing directors base their organization and budget on norms or averages from industrywide surveys. The structure you establish must first and foremost be designed to fit the needs of your marketplace and your employer. Sizing your marketing staff or budget at the 50th percentile of hospitals with a similar number of beds is like buying a pair of pants that is the most popular size sold in the store: chances are they just won't fit.

Surveys and norms aside, there are several factors to consider when determining the most efficacious marketing structure for your organization. They include:

- **The level of competition in the marketplace.** Are you in a head-to-head competition to be the first choice for cardiovascular care in your area? Does your competition outspend your advertising by a two-to-one margin?

- **Management's vision and growth goals.** Is the system looking to increase profitable market share, to reinvigorate its brand, or to merge with another healthcare entity?

- **The organization's complexity.** Is your facility a multihospital health system or an academic medical center?

People make the difference

Don't kid yourself—you need bodies to do the work. Whether they are employed or outsourced, you have to have the right people and the right number of people if you are to be successful. Once again, there is no magic formula to tell you how large the marketing scope should be. When it comes to marketing a health system, there has been a lot of back and forth about whether to centralize marketing resources at the corporate level, decentralize them at the level of the member entities, or use a combination of both (a hybrid model). On the one hand, if the member facilities are geographically spread out, it makes sense to have local marketing representation. On the other hand, some centralization is necessary to ensure the synergy of the brand.

Having the right people is more important than the number of people who make up your department's staff. The required skill sets and competencies should be matched to people who can be both generalists and specialists. The desirable mix of core competencies includes the ability to:

- Plan and set direction

- Synthesize information that can be transformed into strategies, goals, and objectives

- Build consensus and work with internal constituencies to coalesce them around the top priorities

- Set standards and develop methods to determine the effective utilization and management of staff resources

- Manage projects, which includes knowing how to adequately budget for marketing priorities

- Work effectively with internal customers

- Provide periodic reports on key market developments and initiatives

When to outsource

Because they are highly specialized and consume significant resources, certain marketing functions are better accomplished through outsourcing. These functions typically include:

- Call center operations

- Market research

- Advertising

- Printing

- Direct response fulfillment

Marketing versus business development

A trend underway in many healthcare organizations is to differentiate marketing from **business development.** In these organizations, *marketing* is defined as marketing communications: **advertising, public relations, publicity, community relations,** and **special events marketing.** Business development is geared toward relationship marketing and sales: developing affiliations, joint ventures, comarketing agreements, recruiting key providers, establishing institutes and specialty centers, and personal selling. Marketing is seen as analysis and research, business development as deals and implementation. In a number of healthcare systems, there is a certain gray area with the roles of marketing director, director of business development, director of planning, and public relations director. This is not atypical and in fact can work to the advantage of the organization. The fact is that all of these corporate functions—marketing, strategic planning, fundraising, selling, communications, and public relations—are ways of sustaining our ability to achieve the mission for which we exist.

Personally, I believe the "business development" terminology is somewhat vague. A better phrase is "sales and growth strategy." This is closer to the retail world, a world that hospitals are increasingly trying to emulate.

Common denominators of best marketing programs

From my experience helping numerous clients around the country, I have identified a number of best practices for marketing management, employed by organizations that really understand the effect that marketing can have on the bottom
line. Here then are some of the hallmarks of the leading hospital marketers:

Effective marketers are internal and external educators. If nothing else, the
trademark of effective hospital marketers is their ability to manage upward,
downward, across, and out. There is probably no other management discipline
prevalent among hospitals that is as misunderstood as marketing. Your job is
to further the collective wisdom within your organization, so everyone from
top to bottom knows his or her role in building the organization. To become a
marketing proselytizer, take every opportunity to raise the marketing knowledge
bar. One way to do this is to use the intranet to update progress on marketing
initiatives and marketing goals, as well as to assist service lines with relevant
competitor data and consumer/patient preferences. Another way to do this is to
conduct a "marketing university" for department and service line directors. You
can offer marketing education classes online and tie proficiency in marketing
knowledge to directors' performance criteria.

Effective marketers understand the finance game. Achieving profitability is as
much the role of marketing as it is the role of the CEO and CFO. I've known
a number of hospital marketers who are afraid to admit that they can't read or
understand a hospital financial statement. True, you probably don't need to
take courses in financial management to understand the basics of your position.
But it might not hurt to take a refresher course in accounting or statistics.
While you don't need a Harvard MBA to understand the financial health of

service lines and what it takes to achieve consistent profitability, you will be more effective in the organization if you can speak the language of money. Remember, growth for growth's sake doesn't mean much if all you are growing is an unprofitable business.

Effective marketers set priorities and stick to them. Resist the temptation to become an order-taker who tries to accommodate every request for a press release or brochure. Your job is to make sure that staff time and budgets are expended on projects that advance the strategic position of the hospital and its service lines. It is absolutely essential that the marketing department not become a brochure factory or a dumping ground for things no one else can do. Stay strategic, even when they want tactical.

Figure 3.1 shows one hospital's listing of its major service offerings and their marketing priorities, after assessing each service line against criteria such as growth and profit potential.

Figure **3.1**   What to market?

Yes	Questionable	Emerging
Cardio	Senior services	Bariatrics
Cancer	Surgical services	Complementary therapies
Neurosciences	Medical/surgical	
Bone and joint	Diagnostic and imaging	
Diabetes	Rehab and wellness	
Women's health	Transplant	
Emergency/trauma		

Effective marketers don't skimp on market research. Research and development are big in every industry, it seems, except healthcare. Those hospitals and health systems that have significantly invested in researching the communities they serve and the services they offer are also usually the innovators and the leaders in quality and safety. Why? Because they devote more than lip service to learning what will improve the patient experience. As marketers, we can contribute to the organization's ability to set benchmarks and to create an environment that is constantly measuring itself against the state of the art.

Effective marketers are experts on tracking referrals and revenue. For each service line, there is most likely an 80/20 ratio in effect: 80% of the business is generated by 20% of the referral sources. (Of course, this is a generalization. You must find out what the ratios are for your organization's major services lines.) Figure 3.2 shows one hospital's analysis of its diagnostic-related group case mix where the most volume and profit were generated. An analysis of the major diagnostic groups shows that there are six that account for close to 70% of the volume and more than half of reimbursement. These largely correspond to women's and children's, digestive diseases, cardiopulmonary, and bone and joint. While this type of report helps to set priorities, it doesn't mean that the other service lines should be ignored. Rather, it gives marketing a quick snapshot of activity and likely profits. In this case, cardiopulmonary accounts for roughly one-fourth of the hospital's total reimbursement and its discharges, making it the primary driver of volume and profit.

Figure 3.2   The 80/20 rule

MDC	Definition	Discharges #	Discharges %	Reimbursement #	Reimbursement %
14	Pregnancy, Childbirth, and Puerperium	651	14%	$1,961,193	7%
15	Newborns and Other Neonates	601	13%	$808,776	3%
6	Digestive System	594	12%	$4,374,048	16%
5	Circulatory System	571	12%	$3,455,006	13%
4	Respiratory System	569	12%	$3,077,533	12%
8	Musculoskeletal System and Connective Tissue	404	8%	$3,217,367	12%
1	Nervous System	237	5%	$1,362,851	5%
13	Female Reproductive System	166	3%	$1,287,135	5%
7	Hepatobiliary System and Pancreas	143	3%	$1,315,019	5%
11	Kidney and Urinary Tract	141	3%	$770,349	3%
10	Endocrine, Nutritoinal, and Metabolic	123	3%	$552,954	2%
23	Factors Influencing Health Status	114	2%	$1,338,132	5%
9	Skin, Subcutaneous, and Breast	111	2%	$571,790	2%
21	Injuries, Poisonings, and Toxic Effects of Drugs	83	2%	$488,589	2%
18	Infectious and Parasitic	73	2%	$532,473	2%
3	Ear, Nose, Throat	53	1%	$243,662	1%
0	Unspecified	32	1%	$437,439	2%
16	Blood and Blood Forming Organs and Immunological	28	1%	$132,048	0%
12	Male Reproductive System	27	1%	$180,392	1%
19	Mental Diseases and Disorders	23	0%	$127,233	0%
20	Substance Use	23	0%	$75,833	0%
17	Myeloproliferative	14	0%	$151,386	1%
(none)		13	0%	$200,668	1%
2	Eye	6	0%	$15,759	0%
22	Burns	2	0%	$17,804	0%
24	Multiple Significant Trauma	1	0%	$33,659	0%
	Total	**4,803**	**100%**	**$26,729,099**	**100%**

Sorted by # discharges. The top 6 MDCs account for 71% of inpatient volume and 63% of inpatient reimbursement.

Figure 3.3 shows referral patterns for a hospital's gastroenterology program. Here, for example, is a referral map for digestive diseases. This shows that the most important customer group—a group practice of internists and family practitioners—accounts for about 70% of referrals. These referrals should be tracked to determine the revenue specifically generated from the group, and also to identify specific procedures that may be underrepresented in the group when compared to the other 30% of internists and family practitioners who refer patients.

Figure 3.3   Tracking referrals: Digestive diseases

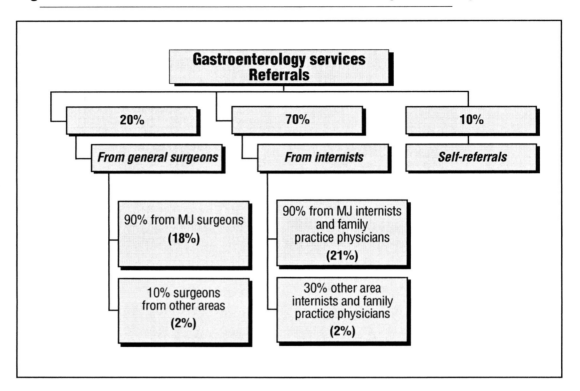

Figure 3.4 shows where marketing interaction takes place for the cardiovascular service line. Volume and revenue should be tracked at each referral juncture.

Figure 3.4   Cardiovascular service line volume flow

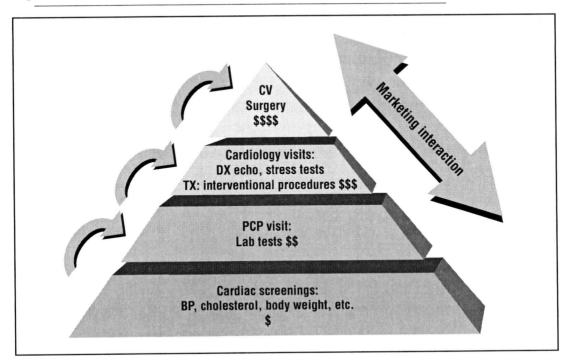

Evaluating the hospital marketing program

As stated previously, there is no universal model for an optimal marketing program. The way the marketing program is organized depends, to a large degree,
on the experience of the director and the complexity of the organization. That
said, all marketing departments, whether for a 50-bed rural hospital or a 500-
bed academic medical center, must have good, solid market research and analysis
upon which management can make sound decisions.

The marketing audit

Over the years, in my role as a hospital marketer and as a consultant, I have learned a lot about marketing structures, core competencies, skills requirements, performance measure, and resource deployment (staff, time, budget). Having conducted numerous marketing audits for academic medical centers, community hospitals, and integrated healthcare systems, I'm pretty well-versed in identifying opportunities to demonstrate the value of the marketing function. A comprehensive marketing audit not only demonstrates the department's value, but also provides an objective basis for justifying further resources.

Some of the questions that a comprehensive marketing audit seeks to answer are:

- Does the marketing department have all of the requisite skills typically needed for effective marketing plan development and implementation?

- Are there deficiencies in the capabilities of the staff and, if so, what needs to be done to improve on or correct the deficiencies?

- Is the most appropriate organizational structure in place for carrying out the marketing program?

- Are marketing priorities set so that there is no confusion over which programs receive marketing support?

- Does the marketing director achieve consensus among internal constituencies about the marketing priorities?

- Does the marketing department provide periodic updates and reports about marketing progress to senior management and clinical leadership?

- Is marketing staff responsive and courteous with respect to service requestors?

- How does marketing demonstrate its value to the system?

- Does the marketing director set overall marketing strategy according to a prospective marketing plan?

- Does the marketing plan have clear goals and objectives, as well as individuals who have been identified as being responsible for achieving these goals within an agreed-upon time frame and budget?

- Does marketing provide evidence of systematic measurement of the initiatives that are undertaken?

- Are resources allocated to the system's entities in a fair and equitable manner according to objective criteria?

- Are external media relations handled appropriately?

- Based on the gravity of a particular issue or situation, are the right spokespeople utilized for press conferences and briefings?

- Is the department achieving an effective balance between the use of outsourcing as opposed to internal production resources?

- Are written communications produced in a quality manner?

- Is the hospital or health system determining its media budget based upon sound strategy and rationale?

- Is the amount of money being allocated to the various media vehicles appropriate?

Although it takes someone from the outside to fully assess how to best optimize a hospital or health system's marketing, marketers can conduct a self-audit (see Figure 3.5) that will give them a snapshot of where they stand within the organizational milieu.

Figure 3.5 Marketing self-audit: 52 key questions

This comprehensive audit covers 52 key characteristics of successful marketing organizations in nine different areas. Score your answers as follows:

In place and at optimal effectiveness:	three points
In place, but could use improvement:	two points
Starting to work on this:	one point

Total the number of items for which you scored three points, two points, and one point. Add together the number of three-point and two-point answers. Consider yourself a leading-edge marketer if the total number of three- and two-point items is at least double the number of one-point items.

		1	2	3
Marketing organization and structure				
1.	The marketing department has an appropriate organizational structure, enabling it to function properly.	❑	❑	❑
2.	The marketing department leader has the same level of clout within the organization that is accorded to the chief finance, nursing, operations, and information officer.	❑	❑	❑
3.	The marketing program is integrally related to, and works closely with, other corporate functions such as strategic planning and business development.	❑	❑	❑
4.	The marketing department staff has all of the requisite skills typically needed for effective marketing plan development and implementation.	❑	❑	❑
Marketing management				
5.	Marketing priorities are set so that there is no confusion over which programs receive marketing support.	❑	❑	❑
6.	The department allocates internal resources according to objective criteria and market demands, rather than to satisfy the "squeaky wheel."	❑	❑	❑

The Complete Guide to Hospital Marketing   © 2007 HCPro, Inc.   **53**

Figure 3.5 Marketing self-audit: 52 key questions (cont.)

	1	2	3
7. The marketing director sets the overall marketing strategy according to a prospective marketing plan.	❑	❑	❑
8. The marketing director achieves consensus among internal constituencies as to marketing priorities.	❑	❑	❑
9. The marketing department provides periodic updates and reports on its activities and progress to senior management and clinical leaders.	❑	❑	❑
10. The marketing staff is responsive and courteous to internal customers.	❑	❑	❑
11. The marketing budget is zero-based.	❑	❑	❑
12. The marketing department competently demonstrates its value to the system.	❑	❑	❑
Marketing functional capabilities			
13. The marketing plan has clear goals and objectives and identifies persons responsible for achieving these goals within an agreed-upon time frame and budget.	❑	❑	❑
14. Marketing provides evidence of systematic measurement of the initiatives that are undertaken.	❑	❑	❑
15. The organization allocates resources according to objective criteria and in a fair and equitable manner.	❑	❑	❑
16. The organization uses an "evidence-based" approach when undertaking marketing initiatives.	❑	❑	❑
17. The department handles external media relations appropriately.	❑	❑	❑
18. The right spokespeople are used at press conferences and briefings, based on the gravity of the particular issue or situation.	❑	❑	❑

Figure 3.5   Marketing self-audit: 52 key questions (cont.)

	1	2	3
19. The department achieves an effective balance between outsourcing and using internal production resources.	❑	❑	❑
20. Written communications are produced in a quality manner.	❑	❑	❑
Marketing information system			
21. Key service-line portfolio analyses are in place.	❑	❑	❑
22. The organization conducts a community attitude survey every other year.			
23. The departments develops maps that track how business comes in the door.	❑	❑	❑
24. The organization conducts a physician attitude survey at least every three years.	❑	❑	❑
25. The organization keeps an up-to-date qualified list of the major physician referrers.	❑	❑	❑
26. The organization conducts a periodic employee attitude survey.	❑	❑	❑
27. The organization periodically updates employer research.	❑	❑	❑
28. The marketing department regularly conducts focus group research to deepen the understanding of key constituencies.	❑	❑	❑
29. The department employs mystery shopping to test service delivery performance.	❑	❑	❑
Service development and pricing			
30. Marketing is involved at the front-end in program planning to assure that programs are designed to meet customers' needs.	❑	❑	❑
31. Marketing advises on pricing, particularly where services may have substantial out-of-pocket costs to customers.	❑	❑	❑

Figure 3.5 Marketing self-audit: 52 key questions (cont.)

	1	2	3
32. Marketing considers all possible fail points in the delivery of a service and advises on ways that services can be delivered more efficiently or effectively.	❏	❏	❏
Marketing planning			
33. The department develops marketing plans for each of the priorities developed with and through multi-disciplinary marketing teams.	❏	❏	❏
34. Marketing goals are clearly stated and objectives are spelled out in measurable terms.	❏	❏	❏
35. Strategic initiatives are organized by target market segment.	❏	❏	❏
36. The department has reliable tracking mechanisms in place.	❏	❏	❏
37. The department conducts an ongoing management development course for service-line managers in relevant marketing topics.	❏	❏	❏
Advertising			
38. The brand message is distinctive, memorable, and expressive of your positioning.	❏	❏	❏
39. Marketing actively manages the brand through consistent message content and uniform graphics.	❏	❏	❏
40. The advertising budget contains an appropriate expenditure for yellow pages listings.	❏	❏	❏
41. The advertising budget includes an appropriate allocation to various other media vehicles.	❏	❏	❏
42. The department bases media planning and buying on sound strategy and achieving maximum continuity in the marketplace.	❏	❏	❏

Figure 3.5 Marketing self-audit: 52 key questions (cont.)

	1	2	3
E-marketing			
43. There is an internal Web board (membership consisting of representatives from the IT department, the medical staff, administration, and marketing).	❑	❑	❑
44. Marketing actively manages Web site communications.	❑	❑	❑
45. The organization's Web site is interactive and allows users to build an affinity.	❑	❑	❑
Sales			
46. The organization has an organized, performance-based, and incentive-driven personal selling program in place.	❑	❑	❑
Media and public relations			
47. The marketing department has an ongoing media training program in place, particularly for key physicians.	❑	❑	❑
48. Marketing holds at least yearly meetings with the editorial staff of the local newspapers.	❑	❑	❑
49. News releases are targeted appropriately and is there more emphasis on meaningful content than on quantity of releases.	❑	❑	❑
50. The organization has in place an evident and effective crisis management plan.	❑	❑	❑
51. The organization has an effective speakers placement service.	❑	❑	❑
52. Members of the management team are involved with community agencies and organizations.	❑	❑	❑

© 2007 HCPro, Inc.

Marketing efficiency and effectiveness

One of the smartest things you can do to earn the respect of your colleagues in your organization is to show them a well-oiled and efficient marketing operation—one that really hums. You can do this by setting the department up as an internal consultancy or agency. This doesn't mean you have to actually start a formal company within the organization (although if you are a part of a huge system, you might consider the idea). Just organize your group so that you relate to the service lines, departments, and other entities within the system as if they were your clients. By doing this, you can keep projects on track and budgets in check, and you will establish accountability. That way, there will be no finger-pointing when a request is delayed.

Managing your clients

Picture this scenario: You are rushing from a meeting with a million things on your to-do list when the chief of cardiology grabs your arm and asks whether you have time for a quick cup of coffee to discuss an idea of his. "Of course," you lie, even though you're due at another meeting in 20 minutes. So you go to the cafeteria, eat yet another unnecessary donut, and ask Dr. Jones what's on his mind. You take notes as he talks about wanting to promote the electrophysiology program, which he feels is underutilized. You tell him that you will meet with your communications manager and will get back to him with some potential approaches next week. "Great," he says. And you rush off to your next meeting.

Later that day, you meet with your communications manager and tell her about your chat with Dr. Jones, explaining that he wants an advertising campaign to promote the electrophysiology program. The communications manager makes a note on her to-do list, which is jammed with pressing assignments and looming deadlines. She tells you she can't get to it until next week. You ask her to see if she can work it onto the schedule this week, because you promised you would get back to Dr. Jones next week with some ideas.

In the meantime, Dr. Jones has forgotten that you told him that now is not a good time to put the message out because the hospital already has an image advertising campaign underway. He left the meeting feeling confident that he'll have an ad by next week.

Your next meeting with Dr. Jones is a disaster. You remind him of your previous conversation, but he insists you promised him an ad this week. He's pressuring you to show him the finished ad by the end of the week.

What should the marketing director have done to avoid this situation?

A. Sent an e-mail back to Dr. Jones summarizing their conversation and confirming the agreed-upon next steps.

B. Told her communications manager to develop a client engagement letter for discussion with Dr. Jones during next week's meeting.

C. Fled into the ladies' room when she saw the doctor coming down the hall.

You may be tempted to say C, and I wouldn't disagree with you. But the correct answer is *both* A and B.

I once had a CEO tell me that 95% of being successful is just getting back to someone who wants something. When I asked what the other 5% was, he laughed. "Hoping they'll forget what it was they wanted in the first place." Keeping customers from feeling ignored or forgotten is the most important tenet of a consulting firm, and it should be a priority of your in-hospital marketing consulting business.

If you work for a large organization and you are appropriately staffed to meet its expectations, consider using an account executive model, in which one staff person is the single point of contact with your client. It's the account executive's role to coordinate whatever is needed to fulfill the request, make sure that the job is done right, and follow up with the client to ensure satisfaction.

How to handle those multiple requests

You know the drill. You have more requests than you can manage, given the amount of time each involves. Both as a marketer and as a consultant, I know what marketing directors mean when they say they wish they had 48 hours in a day to get done what was due last week. How do you say no to those people who carry rank but whose requests are not as mission-critical as others?

Every marketing manager, whether he or she works in a 2,000-bed multihospital system or in a 50-bed rural facility, has the same resources at his or her disposal: time and a finite budget. There's an old saying in the advertising business that everything revolves around speed, cost, and quality. You can accomplish one but not without sacrificing something with the other two. Consider the following:

- Doing it cheaply will reduce costs but could sacrifice quality and take more time

- Doing it quickly will save time but may increase cost and hurt quality

- Adding resources will achieve high quality but can increase cost and time

The most effective means for handling the squeaky wheel syndrome is to use a scoring system based on criteria that measure the priority level of requests. For example, projects could be classified as A, B, or C according to the following criteria:

Priority A projects

- Measurably advance the organization's strategic plan

- Measurably increase profitability

- Have a significant effect on the organization's image

- Cross multiple service lines or affect several departments

- Are time-sensitive

An image advertising campaign is an example of a priority A project.

Priority B projects

- Support a priority A initiative

- Affect one service line

A marketing campaign for the cardiovascular institute is an example of a priority B project.

Priority C projects

- Have little or no strategic significance

- Have minimal impact on service lines

Creating a brochure for the social work department is an example of a priority C project.

Your goal is to focus the department's efforts on the priority A and B projects and do your utmost to keep the time spent on C projects at a minimum.

Maintain a marketing project log and guide

It's amazing how much work the typical marketing department accomplishes. But as a college history professor of mine was fond of saying, "It didn't happen if it wasn't recorded." One of the first steps I take when conducting an audit of a hospital's marketing program is to ask for the project log to determine the number of marketing projects underway and how much time is being spent on them. I estimate approximately one-third of hospital marketing departments do not maintain project logs, another third of departments maintain a log but do not exploit its value as a management tool, and the final third keeps a log and uses it to help prioritize decisions about time management. The value of the log is that it not only gives you a mechanism for tracking work, but it can also demonstrate to your internal clients the amount of time and effort that they have "bought" from the marketing department. This can be very valuable in putting your budget together for the upcoming year.

                    The Complete Guide to Hospital Marketing

You should also maintain a guide to marketing services that can be shared with department heads, service line directors, and others in the organization who have frequent need for marketing services. The guide should provide direction for using the corporate graphics system, when and how to work with marketing staff, whom to contact, etc. Doing this is another way to improve your internal relations and helps to avoid the squeaky wheel syndrome.

Eliminate needless meetings

I remember being at a meeting once during which the person sitting next to me (a doctor) said that if you took everyone's hourly wages and multiplied that figure by the number of hours they spent in meetings on a daily basis at the typical hospital, it would translate into $15,000 a day. That's $3,600,000 a year! And that's without considering the opportunity cost (i.e., what could have been done with the time that was spent in meetings). Now, this may be an exaggeration, but my guess is that, conservatively, half of the meetings that are held in hospital conference rooms, boardrooms, and offices on a daily basis could be eliminated and business would carry on just fine.

There is something very different about the culture of healthcare organizations that makes them so conducive to "meetingitis syndrome." In part, it is the sense that it is necessary to involve people in meetings to cultivate a feeling of shared decision-making. A more likely reason is that it is less risky to form a committee or to call a meeting to discuss something than it is to just go ahead and make the decision. This isn't just unique to healthcare, but it most definitely pervades healthcare management. I can't begin to tell you how many times a marketing director has told me she has back-to-back meetings from 7:00 a.m. until 6:00 p.m., followed by a board meeting at 7:00 p.m. and a 6:30 a.m. meeting the next day. One director had her day so chock-full of meetings that she literally had to eat her lunch while walking from one to another.

I have always believed that 90% of a meeting is social and 10% is business. We are a status-conscious society—being on an important committee or attending a meeting chaired by the CEO lends to stature and perceived power by association. We may seem like we're all business because we have on nice suits and are on our best behavior. Too many meetings are held because no one has ever challenged the reasons for holding them. And let's face it: For many people, meetings are a break from the daily routine. A lot of informal internal communication happens during meetings, and sometimes this is the only opportunity a marketer may get to hear what's happening with human resources, finance, or operations.

Next time you are asked to attend a meeting, ask what specific action is expected to result, or what the expected outcome is. You'll probably get a blank stare, followed by something like "we're discussing the budget" or "it's a standing meeting of the executive council." While there are a number of things you can't control, looking for ways to make meetings more productive and efficient, or to eliminate them entirely, is that more time that can be devoted to bigger priorities.

Summary

- Contrary to most marketing directors' wishes, there are no rules of thumb or "universal averages" for establishing the ideal marketing structure. Yours should reflect the need to counter the strongest of your competition, and may vary year to year depending on your organization's marketing goals. One way to help manage the variability is to outsource specific services.

- Internal marketing is as important as external marketing. You cannot be successful unless you build the internal brand and recognize the interdependence of key clinical programs.

- Marketers must prioritize requests for service. Develop your own prioritization criteria and try to reduce or eliminate those requests that are low-yield in terms of achieving your organization's marketing goals.

- Carrying out a comprehensive marketing audit, in concert with a consultant who is thoroughly familiar with marketing functions and operations, is a valuable exercise that strengthens the efficiency and effectiveness of the marketing program.

- To establish controls and accountabilities, manage your internal clients in much the same way a consulting firm works with its clients.

You be the marketer

You are meeting with your bosses and want to give them an assessment of your workload and how it can best be managed. Included in your workload for the upcoming week are the following tasks:

- Prepare a descriptive brochure for the radiology department

- Conduct market research into setting up a women's health center

- Prepare the business plan for an off-site ambulatory care center

- Plan the hospital's annual heart walk sponsorship

How will you prioritize these projects? What will be your response if you are told that all are critical?

Chapter 4

Branding the
healthcare experience

This chapter will:

- Explain the real value of a brand as it applies to healthcare organizations

- Explain why most hospitals need to differentiate themselves through stronger and more distinct positioning

- Describe the process involved in building your hospital's brand image

Beyond brand differentiation

Brand is everything, right? As marketers, that's what we're always told. But I'm going to let you in on a little secret: Unless you work for a brand giant like the Mayo Clinic, your hospital's brand is probably not very unique. Your position statement—the part of your brand image that expresses how you wish to be perceived in your marketplace—is supposed to differentiate you from your competitors. At least that's what all of the ad agencies say. But in surveys of consumers and patient focus groups that I've conducted over the years, consumers always demonstrate that they are well aware of the difference between a community hospital and an academic health center. They know that a teaching hospital is different from a nonteaching hospital. Many also believe that healthcare services cost too much, and that there is a problem in this country when it comes to health insurance coverage. If you think you can differentiate your healthcare organization by focusing on the fact that you use the latest technology or that your nurses and doctors care about their patients, you are sadly mistaken. If you think that you have devised a unique market strategy when you call yourself a "best hospital" or (for teaching hospitals) say you are the place where doctors learn to be doctors, you are wrong on that count, too.

Consumers have no problem differentiating between a Motel 6 and the Ritz Carlton. We know the difference between the chain retailers K-Mart and Neiman Marcus. There are only two differences, by the way: price point and quality. That's it. We expect the clothes at Neiman Marcus to cost more because they are higher quality than clothes sold at K-Mart. K-Mart doesn't advertise that a retail trade organization has called it "one of the best discount department stores in the nation." And if K-Mart were to suddenly start advertising its new line of first-quality fur coats, those ads wouldn't seem very credible in the mind of the consumer. On the other hand, when Neiman Marcus buys a full-page ad in a glossy magazine for its line of furs, it is credible in the eyes of the consumer. For that matter, if Neiman Marcus started advertising power tools, customers wouldn't rush out to buy them. But when Sears advertises a new line of power tools, it is credible. Why? Because Sears' brand is about satisfying the practical, everyday purchasing needs of consumers, whereas Neiman Marcus' brand is about fashion.

But healthcare, of course, is different than retail. For some reason, even though we know that a community hospital is different from an academic medical center, Americans don't think it should cost more to see a physician at an academic medical center than it should to see a physician at a community hospital. We think all doctors should be equally qualified to practice the highest levels of patient care, and we think all hospitals should be equally capable of providing the best results for their patients.

That's why, when it comes to branding, a hospital must go beyond simply saying "we do the most open-heart procedures," "we have sophisticated doctors and nurses," or "we are a top 100 hospital."

The elements of branding

Definitions of **brand** abound, but I prefer the following:

> *The brand is an organization's means of communicating psychic,*
> *physical, and behavioral representations of its persona in*
> *the marketplace.*

Psychic and physical representations are derived from your *positioning* (how you wish to be perceived in the marketplace) and your *messaging* (what you say in your advertisements and tagline) and include your company logo, graphics, and "lock-up" (how your name is positioned graphically with your logo and mark). Behavioral representations are the many ways that your staff and employees act the brand. In other words, each interaction between a patient and a caregiver or between an employee and a person seeking information or assistance is just one manifestation of acting the brand. In the course of a year, your hospital will have millions of brand representations.

Brand architecture

Most people are visual learners. It's easier to understand a concept that has a memorable image attached to it. Your brand identity will be an important visual identifier for all operating units of the healthcare system and should appear on everything from on-campus signs to letterhead to business cards to billboards and other forms of advertising. It is important that the look and feel of the brand remain consistent every time it appears—that will extend the brand persona and will contribute powerfully to the expectations consumers have of your organization.

In general, there are three classical models of brand architecture, or how your hospital and health system are juxtaposed with your logo and how the overall brand will appear and integrate with the identities of suborganizations, facilities, satellites, service lines, and affiliates. These three models are referred to as monolithic, endorsement, and hybrid.

Monolithic brand model

In this model, the individual members of the system are subordinated to the system name (see Figure 4.1). An example of this is the former Columbia HCA, whose strategy was to create one brand for all of the hospitals in its system—each individual hospital in the system was branded to the parent company. Another example is Advocate Healthcare out of Oakbrook, IL. The primary purpose of the monolithic branding model is to confer positive attributes from the system name to its individual entities so that when a consumer hears the system brand name advertised along with the individual hospital name, he or she automatically feels that hospital is everything the system advertises. A major advantage of the monolithic model is that its branding can be standardized across the system, and member organizations benefit from the system's strong presence. However, a major disadvantage is that if something hurts the system's image, all members feel the pain—as occurred with Columbia HCA when its leadership was indicted for Medicare fraud and irregularities.

Figure 4.1   Monolithic model

Example of monolithic brand model where the system is stronger in sequence and weight than the member entity.

© 2007 HCPro, Inc.   **71**

Branding: A case study

Treemont Health System*, which includes six hospitals and a cancer center in the southeast, serves three geographic areas. The system originally included three hospitals—Birch Regional Medical Center (348 beds), Holly Valley Medical Center (544 beds), and Maplewood Hospital (60 beds).

The system's major competitor is a 443-bed not-for-profit, teaching hospital affiliated with a state university. It is also a member of a regional health alliance, which consists of a number of hospitals formerly owned by another health system.

In 1998, Treemont contracted with a marketing consulting agency to conduct a marketing planning process and help the system overcome brand fuzziness. Each hospital was steeped in its own identity. The challenge was how to preserve the equity each had in its respective community while demonstrating the attributes of being a part of a stronger overall brand—Treemont Healthcare.

Achieving cohesiveness among the medical staff at Treemont's hospitals was a daunting issue. Each of the three communities was extremely loyal to its local hospital, and market research showed that the communities did not have a clear understanding of the value of a hospital that is part of a health system. Focus groups indicated that people thought Treemont was a corporation from out of state that took over their community hospitals, when in fact Treemont was a name that was chosen locally at the time the three hospitals became members of the system. There had been internal competition between two of the hospitals and turf issues over resources, publicity, and marketing. For example, quite a bit of controversy was generated in one community when the system's governing board announced it was exploring whether to consolidate of open-heart surgery services, moving it to the other community hospital less than 20 miles away.

The goal was clear: Build community awareness and positive feelings for Treemont while recognizing the importance of the three communities' pride and psychic investment in their respective hospitals.

The marketing department arranged meetings between the board members of the three hospitals and the system and invited members of the three communities to attend town meetings. Recommendations were made on building both the image of the system and fostering the values that each community cherished with its local hospital.

In addition, a brand/image and service line campaign was developed to promote Treemont and the three individual hospitals. A marketing planning process was conducted, and three service lines were chosen to develop marketing plans: cardiovascular services, neurosciences, and oncology.

The consultation included:

- Market research about consumer perceptions and attitudes to determine consumer awareness of Treemont as a healthcare system and its attributes

- Brand and positioning strategy

- Theme line development ("We're making strong healthcare stronger")

- Public and community relations strategies and recommendations

- Marketing plans for neurosciences, cardiovascular services, and oncology

- Marketing communications, including TV spots, radio spots, print ads, direct mail, outdoor, and Web ads, all designed to demonstrate both externally and internally that Treemont "is us"

The campaign built significant brand awareness and preference for Treemont and its three member hospitals, with a more than 30% increase in unaided awareness of the system and its members within two years of the brand campaign's launch. Relationships between the local communities and the system also improved, and each hospital's board recommended policies for the system board to consider as opposed to the system board making unilateral decisions.

*The names of the organizations in this case study have been changed.

Endorsement model

The endorsement model (see Figure 4.2) is probably the most common form of brand architecture. The endorsement model preserves individual members' equity even though they are part of the system. The individual member is given more weight, with the system given much less weight and appearing "below the line."

Figure 4.2 Endorsement model

Example of endorsement brand architecture in which the individual entity is given more weight than the system.

                        The Complete Guide to Hospital Marketing

Hybrid model

This model combines features of both monolithic and endorsement brand models (see Figure 4.3). The relationship to the system is displayed first in sequence but the individual member is given more weight.

Figure 4.3   Hybrid model

Example of hybrid brand model in which the system is shown first in sequence but the entity is given stronger weight.

The benefits of a strong brand

A strong brand has a number of benefits for hospitals and health systems. For example, a strong brand will give your organization:

- A clear understanding of its brand identity and a straightforward direction for building equity in the identity.

- Pride in the organization and confidence in its future. A strong brand will pull the organization together—its employees, medical staff, volunteers, and friends. All members of the hospital or health system will subscribe wholeheartedly to the new brand identity and what it means for the future.

- A platform from which to drive communications campaigns.

- Support for efforts to build selected clinical service volumes.

- A more coherent and market-meaningful naming process for hospital– and health system–related entities and affiliations, providing a nomenclature and graphics system that will form the framework for current and future relationships and entities.

- An enhanced ability to facilitate capital fundraising efforts.

The process of brand development

In general, there are three phases of brand development: discovery, plan development, and implementation:

Discovery. Before you have your look, your positioning statement, and your snappy tagline, it is essential that you review the most recent primary market research (qualitative and quantitative) and secondary market analyses (market share, growth or decline of service line volumes, etc.). The purpose of doing so is to identify key parameters such as consumer awareness, preference, and determinants of consumer preference and hospital selection. You should also review affiliated and referring physicians' perspectives, as well as other background information relevant to the branding initiative. This will identify what's missing and help you in designing enterprisewide quantitative and qualitative market research for an up-to-date picture of the organization in the marketplace.

In addition, audit all current communications—including newsletters, brochures, letterhead, print advertisements, Web site, and facility signage—for both content message and design elements. If you didn't know it already, this will give you the ammunition to demonstrate the need for the branding plan.

Plan development. The research that you conducted in the discovery phase will help with understanding to what degree your current brand resonates with consumers, physicians, and employers. For example, is your name well known? Are there enough positive attributes for it to be retained, or should a completely new name be chosen? Another decision to make: if going with a new name, should it be a synthetic name (they seem to be cropping up all over these days) such as Alegent, Aspira, Promina, Avera, Provena, Solaris, or Inova? Or should it be based at least in part on the original, more traditional name?

It takes a lot of money and significant community education to change an organization's name. And, at least in the beginning, you'll struggle for even basic recognition of the name in the marketplace, let alone for people to associate it with positive attributes.

When Barnes Hospital merged with Jewish and Christian Hospitals in St. Louis in 1996, the leadership decided to refer to the merged entity as "BJC Health-Care." However, in so doing, all the equity of the name "Barnes," which has a highly regarded and distinguished reputation, was marginalized. Now the entities of the system are marketed directly to consumers, with BJC HealthCare operating in the background as the "corporate endorser."

When choosing a name for a multihospital system, it is important to pick one that is meaningful and real to the marketplace—not just one that satisfies internal stakeholders. The brand must speak to all who directly interact with the health system and its hospitals, as well as to those who never come in direct contact but who are aware of the organization. Most people have never been to the Mayo Clinic, which is the largest not-for-profit group practice in the world and has sites in Rochester, MN, Jacksonville, FL, and Scottsdale/Phoenix, AZ.

© 2007 HCPro, Inc.

But most consumers have a perception of Mayo as a world leader in healthcare. That perception comes from a reputation that has been honed over decades by careful cultivation of patients and physicians and by word-of-mouth marketing and the circulation of favorable stories. (Mayo's marketers will tell you that there is one commandment that rules everything they do: "Thou shalt not mess with the brand.") Mayo does little advertising—it has a trustworthy image fed by its positioning as a leader in clinical research and a facility that manages hard-to-treat diseases.

The brand model that you ultimately choose will be one that is rooted in an organizational structure that grows over time but does not change its mission or core values. Although the model must be flexible to change with new methods of healthcare delivery, it should always express a consistent message that engenders loyalty, trust, and credibility.

Implementation. Much more is involved in brand implementation than simply changing a logo or look. The organization must live the new brand: systems, policies, procedures, and customer service must all reflect what it is that the brand embodies. People don't expect a Neiman Marcus operation when they walk into a K-Mart. They know that at K-Mart they should expect discounted, cheaper merchandise with relatively good quality. But they do expect high-quality merchandise and customer service at Neiman Marcus. Likewise, consumers will expect Neiman Marcus–type customer service in your organization if you position it as the premier provider of medical care in the marketplace. It is vitally important that you communicate the meaning of your brand to frontline and support staff, nurses, volunteers, and affiliated groups that represent the organization to the community.

It is absolutely critical that operations be systematized to ensure that they reflect your brand and positioning. If you are the leader in the marketplace, your communications and operations should reflect that leadership position. If you are second in the marketplace, you want to put forth communications that make you appear to be a leader in the marketplace. And if you are third or worse, look for a tangible way to stand out from the leader(s).

There are three important factors in brand success:

- The brand should be rooted in an organization that grows over time but does not change its mission or core values

- The brand should be flexible to change with new methods of healthcare delivery

- The brand should always express a consistent message that engenders loyalty, trust, and credibility

Positioning: The Holy Grail of advertising

Effective branding begins with positioning (see Figure 4.4). You probably know how important it is to make sure your marketing message is in synch with your positioning. A positioning statement is not a mission statement. The mission statement describes what the organization is in business for, whereas the positioning statement answers questions such as:

- How do we want to be perceived by the marketplace?

- What niche do we want to occupy, given the niches that our competitors occupy in the marketplace?

Figure 4.4
Positioning the brand

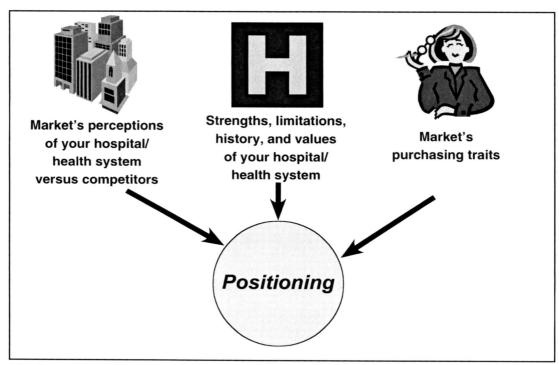

Market's perceptions of your hospital/ health system versus competitors

Strengths, limitations, history, and values of your hospital/ health system

Market's purchasing traits

Positioning

The three major influencers of your positioning are the market's perceptions, your values, and the market's purchasing preferences.

An effective positioning platform can answer "yes" to each of the following questions:

- Does the organization recognize itself—or at least its realistic aspirations— in the positioning?

- Does it name something important to the marketplace, a value that will draw attention and provide a reason to choose the organization over competitors?

- Does it provide a catalyst for the organization to act more consistently to express the brand in action?

- Does it build on actual (not desired) strengths?

- Does it differentiate from preexisting perceptions of the organization (or, if the preexisting perceptions are accurate, does it conform to them)?

- Is it credible and meaningful to the marketplace?

- Can it be backed up and consistently supported?

- Will it tie directly to selling efforts?

- Can it be expressed succinctly and easily translated into a tagline, graphic identifier, look, and tone?

- Does it work internally? Do those who work for the organization buy it?

- Will it help with recruitment?

- Will it help increase business?

That all-important tagline

It's the real thing.
You've got questions, we've got answers.
Just do it.
Good to the last drop.

Odds are good that you not only recognize these phrases, but can also name the brand that's connected to them. You can do this because corporations spend millions in advertising a few little words designed to influence your next purchase of a soft drink, an electronics device, a sneaker, or a cup of coffee.

Taglines come and go. Consider this tagline: "The quality goes in before the name goes on." It was for a company called Zenith. Readers younger than 35 may not know the Zenith brand name, but at one time it was the leading manufacturer of televisions in the world.

True, taglines are not the end-all and be-all of your brand. In fact, a number of advertisers don't have taglines. Brands remain etched in the minds of our customers, not their taglines. But that doesn't mean that an organization shouldn't try to achieve a memorable one.

Healthcare organizations tend to be local rather than national brands. The Mayo Clinic is arguably the closest thing there is to a national brand among healthcare systems. Nobody else comes close. And that doesn't have anything to do with whether they have a catchy tagline.

Still, a tagline does have a specific purpose: to help to cut through the clutter of messages that bombard us daily. Your tagline should be consistently supported in every communication you make. More important, it should embody the spirit of your organization.

Hospital and health system taglines vary depending on what the kind of brand image the organization wants to project. Take a look at the following several hospital taglines. What kind of image is each organization hoping to convey?

- **Columbia St. Mary's hospital in Milwaukee:** *"A passion for patient care."*

- **Exeter (NH) Hospital:** *"The art of wellness."*

- **Edward Hospital in Naperville, IL:** *"For people who don't like hospitals."*

- **Children's Hospital Boston:** "The *hospital for children."*

- **Florida Hospital, Orlando:** *"The skill to heal, the spirit to care."*

- **The Mayfield Clinic and Spine Institute:** *"The science of healing. The art of caring."*

- **Mount Sinai Hospital in New York City:** *"Another day, another breakthrough."*

- **Riley Hospital for Children in Indianapolis:** *"Trust our experience."*

The real value of your brand

Building a quality-of-care/mission-driven culture is certainly helped by a strong, compelling, positive brand that is embraced and understood not only by the nurses, but also by the entire cadre of employees and physicians. Organizations that have been most successful with brand "truthfulness" put their credibility on the line every day. They have learned the ultimate truth: It is in the multiple successes or failures that occur in every provider-patient transaction that credibility is achieved and trust is earned. Improvements in operational efficiency and effectiveness will be realized by the coordinated and harmonious work of many people. When employees work for an organization with which they are proud to be associated, it shows in their service to each other and to patients and makes their statements in support of the brand that much more believable.

A strong and sustained brand campaign will definitely help generate new revenue. Although brand development does not immediately translate into new business, it nevertheless sets the stage for communicating the strengths of the major service lines, which in turn helps to generate volume and revenue.

A branding initiative can also help with nurse and staff recruitment, as well as physician and executive management recruitment. An attractive, credible, and vigorous brand identity will not only help attract people who want to work for your health system, but will also stimulate people who already work there to reach out and recruit others. Recruitment messages should be synchronous with the health system's positioning and key messages. Nothing discourages people from joining organizations more than companies that talk out of both sides of their mouth.

There are three main reasons that branding efforts fail:

- The positioning is not believable

- The brand strategy is a short-term strategy

- Not enough money was spent to build and sustain it

Summary

- To imbue a brand with lasting strength, hospitals must move beyond dependence on third-party endorsements and put forward an image that is meaningful to consumers.

- Your brand model should be flexible and change if necessary, but it should be strong enough to always express a consistent message that inculcates loyalty, trust, and credibility.

- The brand you espouse is not just your logo and your advertising message. It is also the manner in which you conduct business. The brand should be reflected in everything your organization says and does.

You be the marketer

Review your organization's positioning against the criteria listed above. Does it meet the criteria? If not, what will you do to make sure that it does?

Chapter 5

Advertising that connects

This chapter will:

- Explain how to create ads that connect with healthcare consumers

- Give real-life examples of real ads that worked—and ideas that flopped

Eight simple rules for creating ads that connect with consumers

Too often, ads for hospitals and health systems focus on advanced technology or caring providers without really making a direct connection with consumers. It seems all hospitals want to be perceived as "high-tech/high-touch" these days. But in focusing on that goal, we sometimes forget to communicate with patients about serious healthcare subjects in a way that helps them to recognize that they have a need, and that they can come to us for the solution. I've looked at lots of ads that really work—they make a connection with consumers in a nonthreatening, engaging, and memorable way. And, to be honest, I've seen a lot of ads that don't work—they're intimidating, incomprehensible, and completely forgettable. Following are eight simple rules to create the former and avoid the latter.

Rule #1: Make your advertising speak to needs and wants of the consumer

It's a scenario that plays out at hospitals across the nation. Dr. Smith, the area's preeminent neurosurgeon, wants you to create an ad featuring his new image-guided interventional and intraoperative magnetic resonance imaging technology with high-performing computer capability. (How's that for consumer-friendly language?) He wants a picture of the MRI system with his team standing around it, smiling for the camera. Meanwhile, Dr. Clayhorne, the medical director of radiotherapy, is anxious to promote the hospital's newly acquired cyberknife. He particularly wants the ad to mention all of the technical capabilities of the equipment, and wants to show a staged patient lying on the gantry while a huge, scary-looking machine whirs about the patient's head. And Dr. Gaspar, chief of trauma surgery, is clamoring for a billboard that would overlook the area's busiest expressway and show a helicopter picking up a patient from a flaming car wreck. He even has a great idea for a tagline: "West Main Street Medical Center Trauma Center: We'll keep you alive!"

The above stories are not complete works of fiction: they are based on real-life scenarios that marketing directors have experienced firsthand. The point of these examples is not to criticize physicians as wannabe marketers. Rather, it's to hammer home the point that what we advertise must appeal to consumers' wants, and not what we think they want. We must communicate in simple and clear language why a receptive consumer should do something as a result of reading the newspaper ad, seeing the TV commercial, or listening to the radio spot.

What would you think of an airline ad that boasts about how comfortable the seats are in the cockpits of its planes? That's great news for the pilot and copilot. But potential passengers want to know where the airline flies, how many of its flights take off and land on time, and whether it will take care of things if their baggage is lost.

With a subject as serious as healthcare, people are looking for something that connects with an inner feeling, that promises to help them get back to normal, or makes them feel that they have finally found the solution to their problem. Most patients know from their interaction with their doctor and from their own research that they *need* an MRI scan or a surgical procedure. But what they really want is relief from pain, reassurance that they will get better, and a good outcome so that they can get back to playing sports or go on that hiking expedition in Tibet. Yet how many of today's hospital-sponsored healthcare ads do you see making that connection with what consumers want? Too many hospitals and health systems blather about how their hospital is a "top 100 hospital" or crow about being the first in the area with a 128-slice CT scanner. Don't get me wrong—there is some very good hospital advertising out there. But it is not an exaggeration to say that quite a bit of hospital advertising fails to connect with the intended audience.

Rule #2: Understand the decision-making process before you advertise

Retail businesses know that you can attract people to want to buy your product if these conditions exist:

- Consumers have tried the product before and know it works

- They have friends or know of people who had the same need they have, who benefited from the product, and who say it was worth the cost (or wait)

- They believe they have to have it

Retailers know that consumers will impulsively buy a new pair of shoes, a pack of gum, or the latest edition of a tabloid newspaper, but that the decision-making process when purchasing a lawn mower, a new car, or a cell phone—where the stakes and risks are higher if the purchase turns out to be a bad one—is much more elaborate. Consumers like to know that they are getting a little something extra when purchasing one vendor's product over another. And it's not always just about getting a better price. Yes, all cell phones have the ability to wirelessly transmit human voices over long distances. But look! Here's one that also plays the latest hip-hop, accesses the Internet, and ties your shoes!

In order to make a connection with the potential purchaser, healthcare advertisers must be aware of the consumer's decision-making process. It's impacted by the following:

- The consumer's recognition of his or her need for a service

- The consumer's perception or knowledge of the product or service, based upon prior experience or general information

- The consumer's experience with the products or services of similar providers

- The affordability of the product or service

- The consumer's ability to readily obtain the desired product or service

- The consumer's "hot buttons"

How often does the average person pick up a morning newspaper because he or she is looking for the neighborhood hospital's latest ads on its breast care center, or its spanking new cyberknife technology? Answer: zippo! Unless they wrote the advertising copy, shot the photography, or paid for the ad, the average person is not going to go to the newspaper as a primary source for making a healthcare decision. Funny, isn't it, how we in the hospital marketing arena sometimes forget how people access and use information.

Rule #3: Sell the sizzle and the steak—just make sure it's fully cooked

You may be familiar with the phrase "sell the sizzle, not the steak." Actually, you should sell both. In other words, appeal to the target audience's wants and make the product you're promoting everything it can and should be. This is the Achilles' heel of hospital advertising: not fulfilling what is promised. Do you guarantee in the ad for your fast-track urgent care service that consumers will always be seen within ten minutes by a provider or get their money back? Odds are you can't make that promise, because doctors are not always on time, emergencies happen, and a host of unforeseen events can occur.

One of my clients bristled when his main competitor began to advertise their speedy emergency care alternative because he knew it couldn't be backed up. But he was concerned that his hospital would lose patients unless it countered with a similar service. The hospital wanted an ad to go out immediately touting its new fast-track service, even before it had worked out hours and coverage issues. It was two months before my client's hospital had the kinks ironed out, but once it did, the hospital advertised that patients would be seen by a nurse within a set period of time and that any patients who were not seen within the time promised would be recompensed (for example, they might get tickets to a movie, or dinner at a nice restaurant). It took a determined effort to make it all work, but my client demonstrated that if you keep your promises, it will ultimately pay off in repeat business.

There's a general belief in advertising that an ad should never include anything that might possibly suggest that a consumer might experience a problem or difficulty with a product or service. How unrealistic! Everyone knows problems happen, *especially* in hospitals. What they really want to know is: how will you correct the problem if it *does* happen? Wouldn't you think consumers would care more that your hospital has an excellent patient safety record, and care less that you were the first hospital in the nation to get a PET scanner?

Marketing can assist caregivers in achieving these performance standards by mapping out the service process from initial inquiry at the call center to the patient/provider transaction. Some hospitals use "mystery shoppers" to test their services. Others bring in an expert to observe and evaluate potential fail points. However you do it, just make sure that the steak is fully cooked before you serve it.

Rule #4: Don't tell them everything

Remember the cardinal rule of making connections with consumers: appeal to a want and state the benefit. This is an ad, not a statement of capabilities. And another thing: keep copy to a minimum. Your ads should not try to solve all the world's problems—they should get across a single understandable message, and not stray from that message. They should look interesting enough to make someone want to take time to scan them and they should get to the key message immediately.

You might think this advice is obvious, but a goodly amount of healthcare advertising still violates these fundamental principles of effective advertising.

Rule #5: Don't react to your competition unless you absolutely have to

One of my clients thought his hospital should take out a full-page ad to inform the public that the hospital invested more than $5 million upgrading its HVAC system. The idea was to make people less afraid of getting airborne infections and to take advantage of a competitor hospital's unfortunate situation, in which the local media aired a story about its "run-down facilities." But there are reasons not to do this:

- Unless you have had a problem that is being corrected, you are only calling attention to something that isn't the primary decision point for a consumer to choose your hospital over your competitor's. When you shop at the grocery store (which has all kinds of air handling and refrigeration requirements) you don't see a sign announcing that new equipment has been installed to make sure your food is safe, right?

- Playing the reaction game rarely works. Your competitors will remember that you took unfair advantage of a vulnerability and will pounce on an opportunity to return the favor. Play your own game, and you will come out better than if you play someone else's.

Rule #6: Ground your advertising in a communications platform

Have you ever seen a TV commercial—maybe even a very clever TV commercial—and, when it was over, wondered what it was advertising? Have you ever driven by a billboard that you were unable to read? I am continually appalled at some of the substandard advertising for which clients pay good money. And it isn't always the fault of the agency's creative team; sometimes the client imposes requirements in the advertising that muddle the message or that give the consumer an unintended perception of the product or service. I once worked with a small Catholic hospital that insisted a nun in full habit be present in each and every one of their advertisements. They felt this would increase awareness of their mission and their dedication to compassionate care. It was a real struggle to convince them that not only were there better ways to increase mission awareness, but that this could actually hurt their cause. (The agency referred to this as the "subliminal nunsense campaign.")

Every ad you produce must work to support your positioning, and must adhere to the strategy expressed in your communications platform. A well-planned communications platform will keep your message on strategy and will translate the corporate personality in ways that connect with your target audiences. The platform should address the following issues:

- Who is the target audience?

- What is the primary message and what is the "promise" that we wish to convey in the advertising?

- What is the call to action and what are the major benefits that the audience will realize from responding to it?

- Which communications channels work best with the target audience?

- What specific action do we want the target audience to take?

- How will the ad campaign stimulate positive perceptions of our organization and its services?

- What will make the campaign memorable in a positive way?

If you thoughtfully address each of these questions before the creative team starts showing you options, you are guaranteed a campaign that is on target.

Rule #7: Simplify complex information

When I ran a marketing communications agency, I had a creative director who believed that using medical technobabble in an ad impressed consumers and made them want more information on a service or procedure. Needless to say, I did not keep that creative director around for very long. There just is no excuse for advertising that forces a person to consult a thesaurus to figure out your message.

One of the best ways to simplify healthcare issues for consumers is to depict a medical problem in terms of a common, everyday situation. For example, problems with congestive heart failure can be compared to a water pump that no longer draws water effectively from a well. Arrhythmia (erratic beating of the heart) could be explained by comparing the problem to a metronome that is out of sync with the music, or windshield wipers that are too fast or too slow. The basic message—that arrhythmia is serious but can be corrected—is more effectively communicated than it would be if you try to describe an erratically beating heart using only medical terms.

Rule #8: Don't be so serious (but don't try to be too cute either)

In healthcare advertising, there are many opportunities to use humor. But proceed with caution. You can be funny about some matters, but not about others. You might get away with a light-hearted campaign promoting your female incontinence program, your new procedure for treating hemorrhoids, or an antismoking ad. However, an ad promoting your bariatric surgery program by showing an obese woman causing one side of a car to tilt probably isn't a good idea. Humor works only when the person who's laughing at your ad doesn't see him- or herself in it.

Successful advertising that connects

Following are some examples of ads that demonstrate at least one of the rules espoused above. Each carries a singular, position-rooted message that is aimed to appeal to the wants of the target audience.

Figure 5.1 portrays a serious subject—cancer—in a way that grabs the consumer's attention without being scary and without showing test tubes, needles, or other medical equipment. It relates to the feeling of helplessness of people who have been diagnosed with cancer and promises to provide support from diagnosis through treatment.

Figure 5.1

Figure 5.2 focuses on the consumer's wants and the benefits of the service: Bill is a real patient who is enjoying life his way, thanks to heart surgery. This story in this highly-effective ad is told from the consumer's point of view. It contains minimal copy, no jargon, and says nothing about the latest technology and equipment. The consumer can easily understand and relate to it.

Figure 5.2

BILL KNEW WHERE TO GO FOR HEART SURGERY

and he has been on the go ever since.

When Bill Gronow needed heart surgery, he came to Sherman Health. We wondered if he chose us because we're one of the top two open heart surgery programs in the entire Chicago metro area. Or because we've been leading the way in heart care for over 30 years. Or maybe because we have the best outcomes around.

But due to Bill's extensive traveling, we haven't been able to reach him for an answer. And that's just fine with us. And Bill.

For more information call 1-800-397-9000 or visit shermanhealth.com

Summary

As advertisers, hospitals need to communicate subjects in ways that are both highly understandable and that appeal to the wants of consumers. All advertising must be rooted in a communications platform that guarantees the ads will further the underlying strategy.

Chapter 6

New media and the modern healthcare marketer

This chapter will:

- Discuss the role of nontraditional media in marketing hospitals and health systems

- Cite examples of healthcare organizations that have successfully incorporated new media into their marketing mix

---

The age of self-managed marketing

Marketing, the lifeblood of getting consumers to use your services, continues to evolve. Gone are the days when you could put a message out for broadcast over three television networks and capture a huge viewing audience. With the proliferation of communications options, consumers have a plethora of new ways to receive and process messages—and more and more information is directly available when and how they want it.

This truly is the age of "self-managed marketing." Today's healthcare consumers are more technologically savvy than ever before. They want the information they seek to be delivered quickly and in a way that facilitates their encounters with

---

the healthcare system. They are also looking for customization and personalization of information to fit their specific needs. Choice of media is paramount, whether it's in the form of blogs, podcasts, online videos, e-mail, or other formats. Progressive healthcare systems are incorporating **new media** into their marketing arsenal to capture consumers as they search for answers to their specific healthcare problems.

Consumers, the Internet, and healthcare

Study after study shows that consumers increasingly turn to the Internet for information about diseases and conditions. They look up doctors and hospitals online before they pick up the phone. Hospitals and health systems must incorporate online media into their marketing plan.

That said, note that most people do not go directly to a hospital Web site for healthcare information unless they are already scheduled for a test or an admission or are looking for directions to the facility. The sites that people surf are specific to disease or procedure and location and are typically found by using specific keywords such as "cancer" or "heart disease" and the person's geographic location. Therefore, hospitals must embed their Web pages with the appropriate keywords and to link to Web sites where consumers will make their first contact.

As consumers become more sophisticated in their ability to use the Internet to procure healthcare information, marketers need to become more creative with strategies to attract consumers to their Web sites. For example, a print or radio ad could tell the consumer, as part of its call to action, to go to a Web site to get more specific and up-to-date information on a particular test, disease, procedure, or event. Once the patient goes to the Web site, the site could direct him or her to a page that has some interactive element. For example, patients might be asked to complete a health quiz or risk appraisal, be invited to post questions to a physician on the medical staff, or be presented with links to bulletin boards where the patient can share his or her concerns with others who have similar healthcare problems. Even though services do not change all that often, healthcare Web sites offer hospitals the benefit of being able to update this information whenever necessary.

As of this writing, most hospitals are under-budgeting their interactive marketing and have not maximized Internet-based marketing's potential. Many sites provide the basic general facility information that consumers seek, such as directions, phone numbers, visiting hours, departmental information, and general information about specific diseases or conditions that the hospital or system treats, such as cancer, heart disease, stroke, or diabetes. However, they could be doing much more than that.

New media in action

Savvy hospital and health system marketers are reaching out to consumers online and via other new media and using a variety of tactics to get their attention.

The Boston-based Dana-Farber Cancer Institute's interactive Web site allows people to donate to the organization online with the click of a button. And the site allows the facility to keep track of event attendees, collect registration fees for charity runs and swims in advance, and keep donors informed of events at the Institute. A monthly e-mail newsletter is sent out to more than 100,000 subscribers, mostly donors and people who signed up for the e-mail through the organization's Web site, and includes links to news, recipes, and a calendar of fundraising and other events for the institute and its charity, The Jimmy Fund.

The Dana-Farber reports that charitable giving has increased since rolling out the online effort.

The Cleveland Clinic Web site has built a massive library of audio and video podcasts, Webcasts, and articles on healthcare topics. RSS feeds alert users when topics of interest to them have been updated or when the clinic posts new content. A social networking page called "Letters to Tomorrow" invites clinic patients about to face treatments to write a letter to their future selves, describing their experience at the clinic. Cleveland Clinic is also involved with MedHelp (*www.medhelp.org*), an online discussion forum where people can post health-related questions that physicians from Cleveland Clinic will answer. Others can comment about the postings and create further discussion. The strategy helps position Cleveland Clinic as a trusted expert in the healthcare field.

High Point (NC) Regional Health System's Web site features patient blogs centered on three areas of care: cancer, childbirth, and bariatric surgery. Because it was the first healthcare organization to post patient blogs (way back in 2005), High Point received quite a lot of media attention, including articles in *The Washington Post, The New York Times, The Wall Street Journal*, as well as coverage on CNN. The bariatric blog, in particular, has a lot of traffic, with readers regularly posting comments. For a small investment, High Point is able to get a lot of positive buzz.

There is an inherent risk in hospital-sponsored patient blogs, however. What if, for example, the patient does not have a good experience? And any attempt to censor or control the message is easily detected, which could result in an even larger PR nightmare. Keep in mind that there is a delicate balance between authenticity and controlling the message.

The Complete Guide to Hospital Marketing

A handful of hospital and health system leaders are at the helm of the blogo-sphere. F. Nicholas Jacobs, CEO of Windber Research Institute and Windber Medical Center in Pennsylvania, says his blog has helped deepen his hospital's relationship with the community and improved his relations with hospital staff members, who see his blog as a virtual open door, which means they spend less time worrying and spreading rumors. Happy employees make for happy pa-tients, and both can help build positive word-of-mouth buzz.

The future of new media

With new media evolving at breakneck speed, any predictions made while writing this book would surely be out of date by the time it appeared in print. Nevertheless, healthcare marketers are, at this writing, exploring the potential in social networking sites, such as MySpace (*www.myspace.com*), and viral video-sharing sites, such as YouTube (*www.youtube.com*). Blogs by hospital leaders seem to be in vogue these days, and surely this is also an area that hospital marketers will look to expand.

Other types of media have unrealized potential, including handheld devices such as PDAs, MP3 players, and cell phones. Indianapolis-based Clarian Health, for example, gives its bariatric patients free video iPods loaded with information about the hospital's bariatrics program. The video segments include a question-and-answer session with the department's medical director, testimonials from people who have had the weight-loss surgery at the hospital, a video tour of the hospital, and information about the importance of family support before and after the surgery. However, this idea might be slightly ahead of its time. Demand for DVDs with the same content was actually higher than demand for the iPods.

Still, it's easy to see how this idea could be expanded to include all kinds of service line information and other marketing materials.

There are other potential uses for handheld devices, such as cell phones or PDAs. For example, patients could take interactive quizzes (also known as "wizards") to help them determine whether they are candidates for a certain kind of procedure. Hospitals can also use them to guide patients through the informed consent process. For another example, expectant moms could sign up to receive cell-phone text messages that would describe their fetus' developmental stage based on their due date.

Web 2.0 and the active online experience

Consumers—potential patients—are looking online for health information. They're searching for content about their diseases, conditions, or health concerns. All you have to do is post some content about the top service lines at your organization and lure those passive browsers in, right? Well . . . Not exactly.

Today's Internet users are looking for an interactive experience. They want more than information; they want to make a connection. For example, they might be looking for sites that allow them to:

- Research their disease or add their own content to a group-edited database or encyclopedia, also known as a "wiki"

- Communicate with others who share their condition, such as by using a chat room, bulletin board, or blog that allows commenting

                The Complete Guide to Hospital Marketing

- Take interactive quizzes or search a list of symptoms to get possible diagnoses and treatments

- Print out fact sheets or lists of questions that they can bring with them to their healthcare appointments

Summary

- Know how and when to incorporate old media and new media into your communications strategies.

- Use traditional promotional vehicles to create awareness and build favorability with your constituents.

- Use interactive vehicles such as your Web site to keep consumers involved with your offerings and to encourage them to take some kind of action, such as signing up for a healthcare screening, making an appointment with a physician, or taking a health class where appropriate.

You be the marketer

Review the promotional strategies for each service line in your marketing plan. Are there opportunities to incorporate new media strategies? Write down what they might be.

Chapter 7

Everything you ever wanted to know about ad agencies

This chapter will:

- Explain the process of choosing the best advertising agency for your organization

- Discuss how to effectively work with the agency you've chosen

- Explore the challenges of managing internal expectations about advertising campaigns

---

Working with ad agencies

Having served as chief marketing officer at two major healthcare systems and having owned a marketing-strategy and communications agency that specialized in healthcare, I know a little something about working with ad agencies. So trust me when I say that choosing an agency is among the most important decisions that the healthcare marketing professional will make. The right agency can provide you and your organization with the insight and the smarts that will help your hospital jump higher than it could ever jump on its own. Conversely, the wrong agency can ruin your hospital's image. This chapter will discuss the dos and don'ts and the pros and cons of hiring and working with an agency.

Find the right match . . .

You've conducted market research and determined that consumer awareness of your hospital and preference levels are abysmal. Worse, the research shows that one of your competitors increased inpatient market share over the past two years at your expense. You share this information with senior management, and the decision is reached to conduct a consumer-oriented brand campaign. Because of the scope of the campaign, you need to bring in an experienced agency that you can trust—and an agency that you don't have to teach for the next six months to explain just how different healthcare marketing is from other lines of business.

Chances are, the first thing you'll do is develop a request for proposal, or RFP (or request for information/RFI). But that's where you make your first mistake. Before you even think about putting an RFP together, you need to think about what it really is that you want the agency to do. If you don't make it clear from the outset what it is you aim to achieve and how you expect to achieve it, your relationship with the agency will be constantly tested.

The dos and don'ts of RFPs

Unless your healthcare organization is government-sponsored (in which case you have very little control over the structure of the RFP), you should work to keep the RFP from becoming an exercise in useless boilerplate writing. As an agency principal, I have responded to dozens of requests for proposals that weren't worth the paper they were printed on. Here are some dos and don'ts that you should consider when putting a request together:

- **Don't make a big deal over the agency's total billings.** "Total billings" is not a very meaningful figure. Whether an agency says it had billings of $20,000,000 or $2,000,000 has no material bearing on its ability to learn what it is you need to get across to your target audiences. The reason billings is not a good indicator of how much attention you will get is that the figure includes media buys, which may be big for some agencies because media buys cost more in bigger markets, whereas a small market campaign could employ a similar media mix but have a less costly media buy. Also, a few agencies do not take the 15% commission from media reps but instead charge a client service fee and a fee for the media plan, which allows money for the buy to be spent entirely on the buy.

If your intent is to see whether your hospital would be a big fish in a small pond, or a small fish in a big pond, or even a small fish in a small pond, you would do better to ask the agency how many clients it currently has and who it considers to be in the top five with respect to the agency's time consumption. An agency may say it has a lot of clients, but many of these may be "one-off" projects as opposed to agency-of-record clients. (These days, though, "agency of record" doesn't mean as much as it used to. Larger clients, particularly multistate systems, may have multiple agencies working on their lines of business.) However, by asking for the top five, you'll get a good sense of where you would stand among the agency's clientele.

- **Do ask whether the agency has experience in healthcare marketing (not just advertising).** A lot of debate exists among marketers as to whether it's better to bring in an agency that has worked in multiple industries versus an agency that has significant experience in healthcare advertising. The rationale for hiring an agency that has a broad industry portfolio is that the agency will be more creative than one that has primarily concentrated in healthcare. On the other hand, the argument for hiring an agency that has the majority of its portfolio in healthcare (particularly hospitals) means

© 2007 HCPro, Inc.

that there is no need to teach the agency the nuances of healthcare marketing and why it's not appropriate to make light of cancer in an ad (yes, you would think every agency would know this, but not all do).

Tip: If it's a toss-up between an agency that specializes in healthcare versus an agency that has other lines of business beside healthcare, you're probably better off to go with the former. But even more important than the agency's healthcare specialization is to find out how good it is with strategy and planning. Any agency worth its salt can crank out good, even great, creative. But you want an agency that thinks beyond advertising. Some agencies, particularly those that are mostly advertising-oriented, will give you almost no-cost "marketing plans" to get the advertising, which is where they make their money. They will say they are "results-driven." But, as anyone with experience knows, strategy is where it's at. The best way to find out how strong an agency is in strategy—not just creative—is in the interview process, when you can probe more deeply than you can with the RFP.

- **Don't hide the campaign's budget from agencies.** Give them a general understanding of the budget that you are working with. Doing so will allow the substance of the response to the proposal to be stronger, because the agencies will know whether what you are looking to achieve is reasonable based on the available funds. Many facilities are afraid that if they divulge their budget the agency will use all the funds even if the campaign doesn't require it. However, by keeping the budget a secret, you will only receive generic approaches in the proposal. You will always control the budget, so why not let the agencies bidding on your engagement know how big the ballpark is?

- **Do ask how accessible your engagement partner will be throughout the relationship.** The image of your organization, not to mention your own future with your organization, will be greatly affected by how successful your communications are with your agency. If your partner is not as vested in your success as you are, you will eventually pay for it. Make sure this is addressed up front before you enter into a formal agreement.

- **Do be clear about whether it's an RFP, RFI, or request for qualification (RFQ).** It makes a huge difference to the agency as to how you are going to use the information you are requesting. No one wants to go out on a limb and give away their intelligence for free. And client confidentiality limits what an agency will be able to submit. If you want to know the magnitude of a client's campaign expenditures, ask for ranges, not specific dollar amounts.

- **Do give agencies a reasonable amount of time to respond to the request.** If you don't allow sufficient time for agencies to prepare proposals, you are only hurting yourself. Agencies are used to meeting deadlines in tight time frames. However, when forced to respond too quickly, agencies cannot give you their best thinking, and their responses will be overly generic, if you get any responses at all. A reasonable period to allow for agencies to respond to a proposal is three weeks.

The pitch process

You've narrowed the field to the three or four agencies that you are inviting to pitch on site. What should be your primary criteria and key questions for choosing among the finalists? Consider the following:

- Does the president of the agency attend the pitch?

- Do all the key members of the proposed engagement team present and answer your questions satisfactorily?

- Does the pitch address the specifics of your needs?

- How strategic is the agency in its approach to your needs?

- Will the agency be able to work with your style of management?

A word about spec work

Agencies spend significant time and resources preparing proposals and presentations. They must research your marketplace, your competition's usage of the media, spend creative time, and travel to your facility. It is not unusual for an agency to drop $5,000 or more to prepare for a pitch. Although this may not sound like a lot of money to a hospital with a multimillion- or multibillion-dollar operating budget, it is a tidy sum for smaller agencies that often can't compete with big agencies that can absorb these dollars. Multiply that $5,000 by four or five pitches, and you can see how that's a significant amount of money for these smaller agencies.

If smaller agencies have smaller pitch budgets, does this mean you should not consider a smaller agency for the job? Of course not. Smaller agencies can often act more quickly than the larger agencies. They also may be easier to work with, because smaller agencies usually lack the layers of management that are encountered with the large agencies. And, in general, costs are less with smaller agencies that don't have to carry the overhead of a corporate office 1,000 miles away.

Agencies big and small, however, are increasingly opting out of responding to RFPs that do not offer any compensation for the upfront costs involved. To make it a somewhat level playing field for all respondents, hospitals and health systems should offer a reasonable amount of money to each agency for development of speculative creative, if this is an approach they wish to take. However, organizations should not think that a small amount of money defrays the costs involved in proposal preparation and pitch development.

In general, it is best to not go the speculative creative route because it takes time and effort away from strategic thinking. It also is no guarantee that an agency will be able to execute your campaign with effective creative.

. . . And make sure it lasts

Your selection committee has made its choice, and now you are focusing on the relationship that you hope will govern your marketing needs for at least the next few years. The agency has been eager to please, and you wonder how long that will last.

A few words of wisdom for the uninitiated (and even for those who have been down this path before) in the interest of maintaining agency/client harmony: Always maintain your leadership role throughout the engagement and beyond. It's easy for busy marketing directors to fall into the "let the agency decide—after all, they're getting paid" syndrome.

Yes, the agency is experienced and understands account management; if not, it would not have your business. However, it is always the marketing director's responsibility to keep an engagement on schedule, on budget, and on strategy. Remember: You are the engagement partner to *your* client—who just happens to pay your salary. So it is vital that you systematically keep the senior management informed and that you appear in charge at all times. Some agencies are notorious for going behind the back of the marketing director to get an edge on new work, and for ingratiating themselves with those they perceive to have the power to influence marketing decisions. Make the reporting command crystal clear to the agency from the outset—in fact, don't hire the agency without having agency staff members agree to the reporting command in your agreement or contract. Remember: You are the chief image-maker, not your communications manager, and certainly not the agency.

Keep the channels of communication open

Never be afraid to pick up the phone and call to speak with the engagement partner if you are uncertain about anything. If that doesn't lead to results, call the agency's president or CEO. I have seen too many situations where miscommunication or lack of communication at the top has caused unnecessary difficulties that have sometimes derailed campaigns.

Keep things moving!

Nothing is more frustrating to agencies than having to rush to meet deadlines, only to then have to wait for a decision by the client. Agencies are used to turning things around when given appropriate time, and they burn the midnight oil to do so. Stopping progress because a key doctor is in Hawaii and won't be back for two weeks is not something your agency wants to hear, even though you believe the doctor's opinion is critical. Not only is this a poor use of your agency's time, but it also casts doubt on the next time you insist you need the deliverable right away.

Delays in production schedules that are not the fault of the agency can also be costly. Many clients don't realize this. For example, canceling a commercial shoot at the last minute because one of your doctors needs to reschedule may incur not only rescheduling costs, but also a penalty to cover the production crew's time, director's time, and other expenses incurred on the part of the production team. It is always best to have back-ups available and to avoid production cancellations unless there is no alternative.

Pay the agency on a timely basis

Most agencies expect to be paid within 30 days of an invoice. A lot of upfront money is paid for production (up to half the director's fee may be paid in advance), and your agency is not a bank that can afford to finance you. After a comfortable working relationship is established, most agencies are willing to extend themselves and will initiate work on a trust basis so that work is not delayed until internal approval is obtained. But this should really be the exception and not the rule.

Educate yourself in the terms of the business

Get to know the specialists who work in and with the agency: account managers, media planners/buyers, creative directors, executive producers, and production directors. The more you know what your agency representatives do, the more successful your relationship will be. Go on location scouts. Be there during photo and production shoots. Learn the intricacies of gross rating points and when to run a flighted versus a continuity campaign.

Key concerns of clients	Key concerns of agencies	Solution
Does the agency understand how decisions are made in a hospital?	Does the client know how it can cost money every time there is a delay to the production schedule?	Keep decision-making within a small team and avoid using committees.
I only have so much money in my budget.	How much budget is there so we know what can work and what won't?	Agree on how much the budget should be and scope out the campaign based on that.
Why should it take this much time to turn this print ad around? It's not a big deal.	The creative team is committed to a schedule and itinerant requests throw them off.	Map out the creative development and production schedules so there is no confusion if something is changed.

When to look for a new agency

Things have been humming along, the first results of your post-campaign research show that the campaign is starting to take hold, and the agency has done what it was brought in to do. Yet you feel uneasy when communicating with the agency, and you wonder whether it might be time to go back to the market. Unlike "the good old days," advertisers and their agencies no longer stay together till death do us part. There is so much specialization and so much complexity that advertisers today may have two or more agencies working simultaneously on various engagements. The important thing is that the main message stays the same, unless something significant has happened to make it necessary to change.

The signs that it may be time to shop around for a new agency include the following:

- The agency seems to take longer to respond to your requests for assistance. (Could it be that the agency has so much other business that it really doesn't value your business as it should?)

- The creative is stale or—even worse—you discover that the agency has taken advertising it did for another client and simply filled in your name.

- You are working with your fourth account executive in three years (because the others have left the agency or been assigned to other business).

- You know for a fact that the agency, sensing your dissatisfaction, is going behind your back with others in the organization.

Whatever the reason might be (and it could be a combination of all of the above), make sure to give the agency sufficient notice before you elect to go through another selection process. It may be that your telling the agency that you plan to start shopping around is enough to bring the needed respect and service improvement. But don't hesitate to make the change once you've made up your mind.

Using syndicated agencies

No doubt you have received the DVDs in the mail from companies that syndicate advertising, either promising you royalties if you allow them to use your ads to resell to clients in noncompetitive markets or telling you how you can have instant, quality advertising for a percentage of what it would cost to originally produce it. I do not have an opinion on this, other than to say that it could be a good way for a small or rural hospital that cannot afford to advertise to get into the game. However, if you are competing with major players in your market, you need to make sure that your advertising fits your positioning, and the money you spend to do this will be nothing compared to what it will cost you if your competitors steal your platform.

Managing internal expectations

Major advertising campaigns are seductive; organizations can get wrapped up in putting too much emphasis on what the campaign is intended to accomplish. After the initial flush of media attention, marketing directors will begin to worry about justifying the funds being spent on the campaign. I have had clients who have told me how they dread to walk down the hallway because they are afraid a physician or executive will ask how the campaign is coming and whether the organization is beginning to see more patient volume.

Well before the first ad ever sees the light of day, marketing directors must educate the internal community about the purpose of the campaign and its context within the total marketing program. This isn't to say that you should downplay the importance of the campaign out of fear that it will be a failure; on the contrary, for the campaign to be a success it must be viewed appropriately as just one facet of promotion, and not the alpha and omega of marketing. An internal educational program geared toward staff and physicians is a must.

One medical center that I consulted for developed a primer on the advertising campaign, explaining its roots in the new positioning statement and its aim to educate consumers on the importance of the hospital within the community—as a care provider and employer. The marketing department prepared an inservice program and "took it on the road" to departments, medical staff meetings, the auxiliary, and affinity groups. By the time the campaign began to air, the internal community was well informed and capable of explaining the campaign to those in the external community.

Answering those tricky questions

You're going to get a lot of questions from internal stakeholders and decision-makers about your advertising efforts. Let's start with the big one: "Couldn't the money we're spending on advertising be better spent on patient care or on new medical equipment?" Or how about: "We're being told we have to cut costs in our department and that there may be layoffs, yet we're spending hundreds of thousands on advertising. Couldn't that money be better spent on people?" It's amazing that people see advertising as something that is turned on and turned off. You need to make it clear when you answer these questions that advertising is not a tradeoff with investing in clinical care or medical technology. Both are necessary. Money spent on advertising is always well spent if it advances the organization's ability to reinvest in its products and services.

Here's another one: "Aren't we a not-for-profit organization? Why do we need to advertise?" Here's the answer: Our not-for-profit status is a tax designation and is independent of our need to educate and inform our communities of the benefits we offer for sustaining or restoring their good health. Every organization—profit or nonprofit—has to earn enough income to be able to pay its overhead and reinvest in its plant and people.

Another common question: "Why aren't we advertising my clinical service line instead of someone else's clinical service line?" The answer to this question is a long one: A number of factors are involved in determining which clinical services to advertise and when. We cannot advertise everything we do because we do not have an unlimited budget and the marketplace can only absorb so many messages at one time. There are also appropriate seasonal times for advertising. For example, October is breast cancer awareness month, so we may be advertising our women's breast center at that time.

Also, not everything a healthcare facility does is appropriate to advertise. Some services are more direct-to-consumer, whereas others are more business-to-business. For example, for a trauma service, it makes more sense to build relations with the EMS community than to advertise trauma directly to the public.

Besides advertising, there are a number of vehicles in your marketing armamentarium, such as direct mail, public and community relations, special events, the facility's Web site, speaking engagements, etc. We use these in tandem with advertising where appropriate.

And one more: "When will we know if the campaign has done what it was supposed to do?" The answer: There's an old saying in advertising, "When the advertiser starts feeling like the ads are getting stale, that's just about when they start to resonate with the public." The fact is most hospitals try to measure results too early. This is understandable, because board members are often anxious to know whether the advertising was worth the expenditure. Market share movements do not happen overnight, and the campaign should not be seen as a one-time panacea. Rather, advertising should be viewed as an ongoing activity—no different than the organization's continued investment in information technology and imaging. The earliest that a consumer awareness and preference survey should be conducted is one year following a campaign's introduction. Even better is to measure every two years, but keep advertising.

Summary

- Requests for proposals should be prepared to elicit "best responses" from agencies. Don't hide your budget, and give agencies reasonable time to respond to the request.

- When choosing between an agency with no healthcare experience versus one that understands the nuances of this business, it is generally advisable to choose the latter.

- Take charge of the relationship with your agency and always establish the reporting command in your organization.

- Keep to the schedule—for a number of reasons.

- Have a well-conceived rationale for a campaign so that you can answer those who question its value. Keep is short and simple.

- Keep in constant communication with your agency; make sure you are not getting retreaded creative.

You be the marketer

If you don't already have one, prepare a memo with short talking points that answer any questions that the internal and external communities may have regarding your advertising activities. Review your working relationship with your agency. Are there areas that you feel need to be discussed with your account executive?

Chapter 8

Don't neglect your internal customers

This chapter will:

- Explain the importance of internal marketing to the health system's success

- Provide a context for evaluating your internal marketing program

- Demonstrate how marketing can and should be the champion that brings the perspectives of both the internal and external communities to the senior management

---

Internal marketing matters

Have you ever asked someone what makes her feel happy or fulfilled? People's eyes light up when they talk about what they like to do, whether it's hiking in the wilderness, going to a museum with the kids, playing the piano, singing at church, or watching football. It doesn't really take much prompting to get people to tell you what they like to do.

And yet achieving excellent employee morale remains elusive.

With the ever-present threat of corporate layoffs and unemployment, employees can no longer presume that, as long as they do a good job, they'll get to keep their jobs. About 20 years ago a *Time* magazine special report called "Working Scared" chronicled employees' biggest anxieties, including lack of job security, dissatisfaction with supervisors, and lack of growth opportunities, and their sense that the companies they work for only care about making a profit and cutting costs. (Kathleen Lewton, *Public Relations in Healthcare*, 1991, p. 275). The interesting thing is not the report itself, but that it easily could have been issued today. It's shocking how little has changed since then.

Like it or not, these days healthcare has become a tough and sometimes uncaring business. Nursing staff come and go, supervisors talk about achieving targets, and employees increasingly complain about feeling disenfranchised and losing a "family feeling." Physicians' offices are under pressure to see more patients and spend less time per patient. Service line directors are under pressure to increase profitability and streamline costs. Every year state hospital associations cry out that a number of their member hospitals may have to close because of cuts in government reimbursement. Yet employees see hospitals erecting gleaming superstructures and touting their new technology in their advertising.

I have worked with a number of healthcare organizations, big and small, that are challenged by a disgruntled work force. I have found that the common thread in all of them is that employees sense a double standard. They believe that the senior management and the medical staff are often exempt from the policies to which employees are expected to adhere.

Is it any wonder, then, why employers spend thousands of dollars annually on human resources training programs and on consulting firms to help them create happy employees that are enthusiastic, dedicated, and genuinely like doing what they do?

Build your brand from the inside

Internal marketing involves instilling into a company's work force an understanding of its mission, brand promise, and the significance of achieving its strategic goals. Internal marketing engenders adherence to consistency in service delivery and support, and it motivates performance and productivity among work force members.

Building the internal brand is as important as building trust in your external customers. Those businesses that succeed in achieving high productivity and high customer satisfaction have spent significant time and resources on marketing to their employees. In service industries, where the public comes in direct contact with the product provider, customer loyalty is particularly at risk when rude behavior or even indifference is communicated to the customer. Customers evaluate all sorts of cues to good service, and the manner in which employees conduct themselves with their fellow employees is picked up through body language as well as through verbal communication. Retailers long ago learned that the "atmosphere" in a store could make or break a customer's decision as to whether to make a purchase or go elsewhere. It's not only how displays and wares are set up and spaced out, but also how loud people are, whether an employee asks if he or she can be of help, and if an employee can't help, whether he or she offers to get someone or recommend another retailer who can. It's a staple of marketing wisdom that a customer who experiences a negative interaction with a seller will tell up to 10 people about the negative experience.

Having an energized and committed work force, imbued with the values of respectful and compassionate service, will ultimately reflect in enhanced patient outcomes and satisfaction. It will also help retain and attract professionals to the organization who will enjoy working in such a culture.

Maintaining effective internal communications is a full-time effort that requires constant vigilance and innovation. It is more than your employee newsletter and biweekly department directors' meetings. An effective internal communications program must capture the essence of your brand in meaningful ways. If senior management is perceived to be more "do as I say, not as I do," your employees are not going to believe in the message that you are trying to convey to your key external audiences. This disbelief will be reflected in substandard performance and in minor sabotages to your company's image. The effects can be devastating to your public persona.

People emulate behavior that they believe they are expected to adopt. For example, when a family goes out to eat at a nice restaurant, children learn what behavior constitutes acceptable versus unacceptable table manners. In school, children (hopefully) have some teachers who are role models to them. Likewise, in our jobs, we look to our supervisors and how they conduct their daily activities to learn the culture of the organization and the values that the organization embraces.

One of my clients is a midsize Catholic hospital in the Midwest. When visitors first approach the hospital, before actually entering the lobby, they are greeted with a sign that welcomes them and promises to make their stay as comfortable as possible. This hospital has ranked in the top 1% in patient satisfaction for several years, yet the managers were not satisfied with anything less than a perfect score. A person could not walk the halls without getting a feeling of security and comfort. The hospital's mission statement does not state the usual mantra of providing excellent, affordable healthcare (even though the hospital provides this to its patients); instead, it unabashedly states that the hospital's mission is to spread a message of hope, joy, and comfort to all those it is privileged to serve. Contrast to this a hospital where the feeling is cold and not very nutritive, where the employees sense their managers' primary concern is how to contribute to the operating margin. (Incidentally, the Catholic hospital client in the previous example has maintained a healthy net income and operating margin while encouraging a supportive environment for employees.)

As marketers, we don't have to work in a healthcare organization that is affiliated with a religion to be able to build an internal culture that embodies customer service excellence, courtesy, and respect for individuals. The key is to impress upon your colleagues how important it is that living the brand start at the top and that, if it does, it will replicate its way through the ranks.

While HR has traditionally been the linchpin for monitoring and managing internal communications, the marketing department has an increasingly pivotal role to play in internal marketing. It is the integrating unit in the organization because it has significant interface with both internal and external communities. Marketing must translate the culture of the organization for both communities and is in the best position to bring the perspectives of both to senior management.

The internal marketing audit

In the hospital or health system, each department is a buyer or a seller of services. The pharmacist "sells" services to the nursing unit on third floor, the operating suite buys services from central supply, radiology sells services to the operating room, and so on. One way to build a strong internal service culture is to have each department of the hospital chart out whom it depends upon to carry out its role and who in turn depends upon the department to carry out its role. The chart that results from this exercise helps departments become better at reducing the number of hand-offs and dissatisfaction that can occur between internal sellers and buyers.

An internal marketing audit is the first step that marketing can undertake to determine what should be done to improve internal communications. An internal marketing audit involves several steps.

- Conduct an inventory of all written and electronic internal communications, including:

    - Print publications (e.g., employee newsletters, collateral, flyers, magazines)

    - Videos

    - Displays/bulletin boards

    - Intranet communications

    - Employee handbooks and policy manuals

    - Way-finding signage

- Review the results of the most recently conducted employee climate survey (if there is no survey, conduct one in order to obtain a baseline against which subsequent surveys will be measured following implementation of internal communications strategies and tactics). Assess each of the communications vehicles against evaluative criteria, which will include:

- Primary purpose of the particular vehicle

- To whom the vehicle is directed

- Principal messages

- Strengths and weaknesses of the vehicle

- Interview representatives from various departments of the hospital, as well as selected physicians and members of the executive leadership. Issues to be probed include:

  - Type of information interviewees would like to have and how they want to receive it

  - Perspectives on the existing communications vehicles and their relative value to performing their job

- Conduct a series of focus groups with employees to develop further what is learned from the survey and the interviews and to test interest in potential changes and undertakings.

Following are some ways that healthcare marketers can build an effective internal marketing program:

Develop an educational program to achieve brand congruity. Much more than simply changing a logo or look is involved in brand implementation.

The organization must live the new brand, meaning that systems, policies, procedures, and customer service must all reflect what it is that the brand embodies. As noted earlier, people don't expect a Neiman Marcus experience when they shop at K-Mart. At K-Mart, they expect discounted and cheaper merchandise with generally good quality. But they do expect high-quality merchandise and customer service at Neiman Marcus. Likewise, consumers will expect Neiman Marcus–type customer service in an organization that positions itself as the premier provider of medical care in the marketplace. It is vitally important to communicate the meaning of the brand among frontline and support staff, nursing, volunteers, and affiliated groups that represent the organization to the community.

Sponsor an "all star" spotter program. The most tangible way to achieve behavioral congruity with the brand is to reward employees when they demonstrate desirable behavior. A spotter is any employee who witnesses outstanding customer service, job performance, or simple friendliness to a patient, visitor, or fellow employee—it doesn't need to be a heroic act, just something that makes someone else's job easier or that helps a visitor or patient. Such acts are then rewarded. Rewards should be generous and not just a free lunch at the cafeteria. The great thing about the spotter's program is that employees never know who is a spotter—so they act as if everyone is.

Maintain an internally and externally focused call center. Healthcare enterprises tend to lose sight of the fact that employees are consumers too and are often just as in need of answers. Call centers aren't just for answering questions or helping people from outside the organization; they can also be sources of information and support for persons on the inside, as well.

Employees may need information on educational classes and appointment scheduling just as much as the outside consumer.

Use an intranet to keep employees engaged in the exchange of ideas that can strengthen the corporate vision and culture. Employees have a wealth of information that is rarely tapped. Today's healthcare organizations must clear obstacles and provide an open channel of communications to connect with employees regarding the company's goals. For example, employees could respond instantly to another employee's question about how to handle a problem with which a patient's family member has asked for help. Using the intranet in this way can create a mechanism by which employees can share ideas and assist one another in real-time.

Engage physicians and other nonemployed groups who are integral to the success of the enterprise. Major companies, such as Ford and Proctor & Gamble, don't just require their employees to adhere to their culture. They also make it a requirement of their contractors and subcontractors. Both employed and independent physicians on your medical staff represent your hospital on a daily basis and need to abide by the same rules as employees when it comes to courtesy, respect, etc. Many hospital executives exclude physicians from internal marketing because they fear physicians will share competitive information with rival hospitals. In all my years of consulting, I have never seen anything that has been communicated to physicians come back and bite the hospital. Rarely is anything communicated that would compromise the ability of the hospital to build market strength, establish a new clinical program, or undertake a strategic initiative.

Ideally, it is best that an internal marketing course be developed for both physicians and service line leaders together, using an outside consultant to facilitate. The course should cover the interaction of branding and business development in building successful clinical programs, and internal marketing and its effect on patient referral processes and patient care processes. Or a separate course can be developed for physicians. Either way, it is essential to engage your medical staff in your internal marketing initiatives.

Create talking points aids. A very simple printed piece can be put together for hospital managers to use in presentations to employees to ensure that everyone receives the same message. This can also be accomplished via in-person Power Point presentations and can be loaded on the intranet for employees' future reference.

Internal marketing case study

Facility: An academic medical center in the Chicago metropolitan area.

Problem: Low morale and diminished productivity at the call center; lack of internal awareness of programs and services available within the medical center.

Background: AMC University Hospital is a major academic medical center located in the Chicago area. It includes a medical school, a teaching hospital, and a nursing school. The medical center's growth over the past 10 years has put a significant strain on the organization's ability to keep employees informed of developments in clinical care, education, and research. Of even greater concern, however, were results of an employee survey that indicated that close to 35% of employees couldn't name the medical center's key programs.

Associates at the internally managed call center felt that they could not spend significant time on calls because of other duties, including report development and researching call inquiries.

Approach and solution: After analyzing the number and types of calls that were being managed at the call center, and after making trips to other academic medical centers that have successfully managed similar issues, the director of marketing, working with the director of IT, chose a solution that used both communications and software. Call center associates met with the various departments within the health system to learn more about programs and services and to meet key people. This also provided a valuable opportunity for department directors to learn more about the important role that the call center plays as the first contact point for many consumers. The software solution came in the form of technology that allowed the hospital to record a greeting in the associates' voices. This allowed the call center associates a few extra seconds to prepare for the caller's request. It also helped to save their voices so that they would not sound tired or unenthusiastic as the day wore on.

Because of its central role as an information source, the call center was able to access and provide information for employees via the intranet to promote internal knowledge of recent developments in programs and services.

Summary

- Internal marketing is a full-time effort. To the extent that employees tie their individual role to the success of the organization, customer satisfaction and positive outcomes will soar.

- Internal marketing starts at the top. The work force takes its cues from the culture that senior management condones.

- Marketing has an important role in ensuring synergy between external and internal communications and in devising communications vehicles that cultivate 360-degree communication among employees.

You be the marketer

Do you have an internal marketing program in place? If you do, how well is it working and what can you do to make it more successful? If not, what will you do to prepare one?

Chapter 9

The future of healthcare marketing

An out-of-this world scenario?

This is the chapter in which we take stock of where we've been and consider where we are heading in the context of healthcare, not just hospital-based marketing. If I were sitting at my computer several years from now, working on the fifth edition of this book, what might I be writing about? Here's one possible timeline:

2015: Patients can directly and wirelessly book their own rooms in hosphotels (what used to be called "hospitals") from their home networks. They can choose the time frame in which to schedule a procedure, much like hotels let patrons order time ranges for room service. They can even book a room that is "pet-friendly."

2019: Consumers can design their own healthcare treatment plans and solutions, evaluating their options and electronically sharing techniques and results with other consumers around the world with similar experiences. They can even interact with their medical provider (who can be anywhere in the world) through holographic and virtual medical intervention.

2022: Drugstores offer diet treatment products that automatically reduce body mass overnight without adverse side effects, making bariatric surgery for overweight persons a barbaric practice of the past. The products can be ordered via the galactonet (we now have wireless connectivity with that new planet, which was discovered in 2020).

2025: A new invention, the painometer, provides neuromapologists (a new subspecialty of neurology) with objective measurement of pain, thus doing away with the old "tell me, on a scale of 1–10, how much does it hurt?" measurement, and they are now able to accurately pinpoint the specific nerve fibers that are causing pain. This greatly increases patient satisfaction scores.

If you think the above scenarios are out of this world, think again. Okay, there's no such thing as a galactonet. But more and more hospitals are making customer service a part of their marketing strategy, offering concierge services that pick up patients' dry cleaning, for example. Some nursing homes already allow patients to have pets. Walgreen's now offers many self-diagnostics. Several national drugstore and grocery chains are opening new patient clinics. And one progressive medical center in the Midwest is experimenting with a program that allows consumers to check into their hospital room without going through admitting. So in many respects, the future is already here.

Marketing is where the action is

Whether they know it or not, when it comes to the future of healthcare delivery, hospital and health system marketers are in the driver's seat. As consumers become more knowledgeable (which is happening, thanks in part to the vast amount of information available on the Internet), more responsible for maintaining a healthy lifestyle (as they are through employers' increasing restrictions on unhealthy behaviors and incentives to adopt healthier lifestyles), and more sensitive to the cost that accompanies their use of healthcare resources (as they are through health savings and reimbursement accounts and increasing out-of-pocket expenditures), healthcare marketers will rise in their role as shapers of the next wave of products and delivery.

The exciting news is that information systems—electronic health records, remote linkups of disparate sites where patients receive care, and the explosive potential for clinical information and service delivery via computer networks—will allow consumers greater control of their personal health issues. The future of healthcare marketing is inextricably tied to information systems technology and to one-on-one relationship building. And as I said in the introduction, it is the healthcare marketers of tomorrow who will keep challenging the old ways and will reinterpret healthcare marketing for the next wave of healthcare marketers to interpret yet again.

Best of luck!

Glossary

Advertising: Sponsored communications through which an advertiser pays to positively persuade or influence individuals or groups regarding its services.

Brand/branding: The process of differentiating an organization from its competition, through physical graphics, messaging, and behavior.

Business development: A focused area of marketing that is geared toward building sales and relationships that foster growth, such as joint ventures with physicians or other healthcare entities.

Community relations: A form of public relations that seeks to engender good will with the public and community organizations through various programs and services. Examples: health fairs, participation on boards of local agencies.

Customers: Individuals and groups of individuals who utilize our services either to enhance delivery of their own services or to satisfy a healthcare-related need. Customers can be businesses or consumers.

Diagnostic related groups: Groupings of similar diagnostic and treatment services that are paid at a fixed rate (with certain adjustments) by Medicare and other payers.

Direct marketing: The activities that directly influence the sale of goods and services through face-to-face selling, direct mail, telemarketing, direct-action advertising, catalogue selling, etc.

Focus groups: A form of primary research that involves a facilitator and a subject group that is invited to discuss issues from which the sponsor of the focus group desires to gain insight.

Internal marketing: The series of activities that are designed to inculcate employee allegiance to the brand, and to ensure quality and consistency in service delivery and support.

Marketing (general): The process by which the producer or seller of a good or service learns what current or potential customers need. It includes all the efforts involved in fulfilling these needs. It involves an exchange relationship between a buyer and seller in which the buyer makes a price/value assessment, resulting in either acceptance or rejection of a good or service.

Several factors interplay in the development of this exchange relationship between the provider and consumer:

- The consumer's recognition of his or her need for a service

- The consumer's perception or knowledge of the product or service, based upon prior experience or general information

- The consumer's experience with the products or services of similar providers

The Complete Guide to Hospital Marketing

- The provider's understanding of the consumer's needs or wants

- The affordability of the product or service

- The consumer's ability to readily obtain the desired product or service

Marketing (healthcare): The process of educating ourselves as to the healthcare wants and needs of our potential customers, and, based on the knowledge we gain, educating our customers and offering them valued services that fulfill their needs when and where they need those services.

Marketing audit: An assessment of marketing structure and functions that identifies opportunities for strengthening and optimizing marketing programs and resources.

Marketing information system: The systematic collection of data for interpretation and analysis for supporting decision-making.

Marketing mix: The interaction of the Four P's—product, place, price, and promotion—that works to attract potential customers and sustain customer satisfaction.

Marketing plan: A written document for selling products and services. It is composed of an analysis of the current marketing situation, opportunities and threats, target groups, goals and objectives, strategies, resources, and action steps.

Market segmentation: The process of breaking the total potential buyers of a service into segments that may be defined geographically, economically, or behaviorally.

Market share: An organization's take of all of the business within a defined parameter (e.g. a certain geographic area or a demographic category).

Marketing strategies: The specific approaches taken to achieve marketing goals.

New media: Refers to nontraditional media vehicles for attracting potential customers, including Internet-based communications and personalized electronic communications through digital media such as DVDs, personal digital assistants, etc.

Positioning: Refers to how an organization wishes to be perceived in the marketplace. A position is achieved by associating the benefits of a brand with the needs or lifestyle of the targeted audience.

Primary market research: Involves the seeking of intelligence that is generated from original sources such as household telephone surveys, direct mail surveys, focus groups, mall intercepts, and other means of obtaining unpublished information.

Public relations: The form of promotion that seeks to make use of publicity and other forms of communication to influence the feelings, opinions, or beliefs about an organization, and its products and services.

Reimbursement: The amount that hospitals are paid by government-sponsored and private insurers for services rendered, as opposed to being paid for full charges. Typically a hospital is subjected to a contractual adjustment, so that the amount that is paid is net of the contractual adjustment and other costs that may be disallowed per contract.

Return on investment (ROI): In marketing parlance, this simply refers to coverage of an investment in marketing a service or program. For example, if a marketing effort has a cost of $100,000 and the revenue that is generated from the effort is $110,000, then the marketing effort had a 10% return on the initial investment.

Secondary market research: Research involving the use of already existing information that was compiled for a particular purpose.

Service line: A management structure in which the production and service components involved in the delivery of a care process (e.g. cardiac services) are organized under the direction of a manager and medical director.

Special events: Related to community relations, these are activities undertaken by an organization that allow for an interested party to learn more about the organization or to use a service of the organization. Examples include healthcare screenings, award ceremonies, conferences, and speakers programs.